THE HAIR PULLING "HABIT" AND YOU

HOW TO SOLVE THE TRICHOTILLOMANIA PUZZLE

Revised Edition

Ruth Goldfinger Golomb, M.Ed., LCPC
Sherrie Mansfield Vavrichek, LCSW-C, BCD

Writers' Cooperative of Greater Washington
Silver Spring, Maryland

10 9 8 7

Published by   Writers' Cooperative of Greater Washington
                  P.O. Box 10550
                  Silver Spring, Maryland   20914-0550

This book was printed and bound by United Graphics, Inc., Mattoon, IL

Illustrations by Uri Yokel and Emily Condon-Douglas
Cover design by Donna Rudolph of AlphaGraphics

Publisher's Cataloging-in-Publication
(Provided by Quality Books, Inc.)

Golomb, Ruth Goldfinger.
   The hair pulling "habit" and you : how to solve the
trichotillomania puzzle / Ruth Goldfinger Golomb,
Sherrie Mansfield Vavrichek ; [illustrations by Uri
Yokel and Emily Condon-Douglas]. -- Rev. ed.
      p. cm.
   Includes bibliographical references.
   SUMMARY: Shows young people how to break the
compulsive hair pulling habit by identifying trigger
situations, developing resistance strategies, charting
progress, modifying environments, motivating themselves,
and staying with the program. Advice for parents and
therapists is appended.
   LCCN: 00-106855
   ISBN: 0-9673050-2-0

   1. Compulsive hair pulling--Juvenile literature.
I. Vavrichek, Sherrie Mansfield. II. Title.

RC569.5.H34G65 2000   616.85'84
                             QBI00-724

To our husbands and children
With love:

Jon, Nikki, and Jacob
Bruce, Diane, and Julie

Disclaimer

This book is designed to provide information regarding the subject matter covered. It contains only the information available to the authors at the time of printing. Furthermore, it is sold with the understanding that the authors and publisher are not engaged in rendering psychiatric, psychological, medical, or other professional services to the reader. If such services are required, they should be sought from a competent, licensed professional in the appropriate field.

Every effort has been made to make this book as complete and accurate as possible. However, there may be typographical errors or mistakes in content. In addition, specific needs and circumstances may cause part or all of the material presented in this book to be inappropriate for certain individuals. Therefore, this text should be used only as a general guide and not as the ultimate source regarding trichotillomania and its treatment.

The purpose of this book is to provide information only. No guarantees, either explicit or implicit, are made regarding the effectiveness of this program for any individual. Neither the authors nor the Writers' Cooperative of Greater Washington shall have liability or responsibility to any person or entity with respect to any loss or damage or any other problem caused, or alleged to have been caused, directly or indirectly, by the information contained in this book.

TABLE OF CONTENTS

ACKNOWLEDGEMENTS

The authors are extremely grateful to the many medical and mental health professionals with whom we have collaborated over the years, and from whom we have learned so much. In particular, we would owe a debt of gratitude to Dr. Charles Mansueto, Director of the Behavior Therapy Center of Greater Washington (BTC), for first giving us the opportunity to work with people suffering from trichotillomania, and for including us in the process of learning more about the nature of this disorder. Dr. Mansueto, Dr. David Keuler (who offered many valuable editorial suggestions), Maddy Cleveland, and our other colleagues at BTC gave us much support and good advice throughout the project. We would like to thank them all.

Christina Pearson, founder and Director of the Trichotillomania Learning Center (TLC), has been a source of inspiration and encouragement to us during our many collaborations over the years, including our work on this book. Under her leadership and that of the organization's Science Advisory Board, TLC has become an invaluable resource to professionals as well as to people suffering from trichotillomania through its information services, newsletters, research efforts, conferences, and retreats.

We would also like to thank Xaviar Castellanos, MD, Fred Penzel, PhD, Larry B. Silver, MD, Melinda Stanley, PhD, and Susan Swedo, MD, for reviewing our manuscript, and for their insightful and knowledgeable comments and recommendations.

Our husbands, Jon and Bruce, gave us tremendous support and excellent advice throughout the entire project. Diane Vavrichek, also a family member, deserves a special word of thanks for her extremely valuable editorial and word-processing services.

Our words of appreciation would not be complete without also mentioning Uri Yokel and Emily Condon-Douglas, our illustrators. Their whimsical and creative illustrations added the visual components so vital for the understanding and enjoyment of this book. We also would like to thank Donna Rudolph, who designed our cover, for her talented guidance and for her patience.

Finally, we thank our clients for being our most valuable teachers. Without their patience, determination, and trust this book would not have been possible.

Ruth Goldfinger Golomb
Sherrie Mansfield Vavrichek

September, 2000

PREFACE

(This Preface gives some background information about this workbook. Young readers who find it boring can just skip it!)

The Hair Pulling "Habit" and You, Revised Edition, is an updated guide for controlling chronic hair pulling -- a habit known as trichotillomania. It was written primarily for young people between 10 and 16 years of age. However, the authors hope that mental health professionals, parents of children with trichotillomania, and older adolescents and adults who suffer from this disorder will also find this book to be a useful resource.

The treatment approach presented here is based on a framework developed in the late-1980's when Dr. Charles Mansueto, Director of the Behavior Therapy Center of Greater Washington (BTC), began working with a number of patients with trichotillomania. These patients had been referred to BTC by the National Institute of Mental Health (NIMH).

Little was known about trichotillomania at that time, but there were many theories regarding its nature. Some researchers saw it as a form of a condition known as obsessive-compulsive disorder. Others viewed it as instinctive grooming behavior gone out of control. Still others suggested that the problem resulted from a disorder of brain function or was a symptom of underlying psychological problems. In contrast, many people saw trichotillomania as merely a "bad" habit.

As Dr. Mansueto began working with the NIMH-referred patients, it became clear that the treatments inspired by existing theories produced only limited success in alleviating hair pulling. There was room for new ideas on the subject, and these patients provided a unique opportunity to take a fresh look at a largely unsolved problem.

Dr. Mansueto began to systematically examine various characteristics of patients with trichotillomania, paying particular attention to each sufferer's internal experiences. Over the past several years, a more complete picture has emerged, indicating that the disorder involves complex patterns of habits, sensations, emotions, thoughts, and environmental triggers. With this understanding, Dr. Mansueto and his colleagues have developed an assessment and treatment approach based on each client's unique profile. Through their years of work at BTC, the authors have been closely involved in the development of this model, and have been successful in using it to treat people of all ages who suffer from trichotillomania.

Early on in their work, the authors became aware of the somewhat different needs of younger clients, who comprise a significant share of this client population. Consequently, the authors have adapted and modified the approach for use with children and teenagers. This book, which can be used as a self-help program for children and teens (and yes, adults can use it, too), as well as a guide for parents and therapists, is the outcome of those efforts.

CHAPTER 1

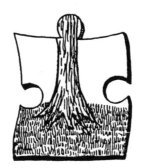

LEARNING ABOUT TRICHOTILLOMANIA

INTRODUCTION

If you are reading this book, you are probably a young person who pulls out hair from some part of your body. This problem is called trichotillomania--also called "trich" (pronounced "trick") or TTM-- and having it has most likely caused you a great deal of frustration and embarrassment. Here is some information about trich that you might find interesting:

People with trichotillomania generally pull hair from their heads, eyelashes, or eyebrows, although some pull from their legs, arms, or pubic areas. Some people just throw away the hair, but many people "play" with it after they pull. They might, for instance, roll the hair between their fingertips, rub or touch the hair against their face or skin, or look at the pulled hair very closely. Others bite or swallow the hair. A person may do one, two, or all of these things once hair has been pulled. Everyone's hair pulling behavior is unique.

Trichotillomania is usually reported by girls and women, although boys and men suffer from it as well. While some people begin pulling their hair when they are between 9 and 14 years of age, it can start at younger or older ages. Trichotillomania is not as rare as you might think. Over 5,000,000 people in the U.S. alone have trich, and millions more may suffer from it throughout the world!

IS TRICHOTILLOMANIA LIKE A "BAD HABIT"?

Some people think that trichotillomania is like a "bad habit." But is it really?

A habit is something that you do so often and automatically that you do not even think about it. Some habits are thought of as "good" habits, such as brushing your teeth. Some are thought of as "bad" habits, for example, throwing your towel on the floor after a shower rather than hanging it up. Some are just things that you might do that are neither good nor bad, like putting your right sock on before your left when you get dressed. However, once a habit is established, it can become so **automatic** and **strong** that a person can have a very hard time stopping, even when she really wants to.

There are certain "body-focused" behaviors that are sometimes thought of as habits because they are repetitive and automatic. These behaviors often have to do with some of our senses (touch, smell, taste, sight, and/or hearing). Many babies and young children, for instance, suck their thumbs. Some kids, teens, and adults bite their fingernails, pick at their skin, chew on their lips, or bite the insides of their cheeks. Twisting, twirling, or pulling out hair are often thought of as body-focused "habits," too.

Sometimes hair pulling and other body-focused "habits" go away by themselves. In other cases, people are able to limit these activities so that they do not cause them harm or embarrassment. But for some people, hair pulling becomes a problem. How can you tell if your hair pulling behavior has become a problem? Here are some of the signs:

- You are hurting yourself or visibly changing the way you look;
- You spend so much time pulling your hair that it interferes with other activities;
- It causes you embarrassment or worry; and/or
- It creates tension or arguments in the family.

When hair pulling becomes a problem, it is called "trichotillo-mania." No one knows exactly why TTM affects certain people and not others. But, some doctors have noticed that for a number of people with this problem, a certain part of the brain works a little bit "differently" when it comes to hair pulling. For some of these people, the brain may send or receive certain "signals" which may **stimulate** pulling. For other people, when a hair is pulled, instead of the brain sending the message, "Ouch! I won't do that again!" it sends the message, "Ooh. That feels kind of interesting." In either case, because of this "difference," hair pulling can quickly move from being an occasional, harmless behavior to a disfiguring prob-lem.

So, is trichotillomania a habit? The answer is "sort of." For some people hair pulling may be just like other body-focused "habits." For others it is not. People pull their hair for may different reasons.

This book will help you learn more about your hair pulling problem and what you can do about it!

HOW TO USE THIS BOOK

If you have struggled with hair pulling over a long period of time, you might wonder if you will ever be able to better control and manage trich. Well, as two mental health professionals who have helped hundreds of people with TTM, we can tell you that the approach that is used in this book **can** help most people. And you will be happy to know that you have already taken the first two steps! First, you have realized that you have a problem. Second, you have started reading this book! As you continue reading, you will learn how to take the remaining steps, one at a time.

To begin this program, we recommend that you **read the entire book all the way through**. Then, go back to the beginning and carefully go through each chapter. By **following the steps in each chapter**, you will soon have the tools you will need to help you gain better control over trich.

Although you are the person who will be responsible for doing the assignments, your parents' involvement may be very useful, so please ask them to read this book, too, including the Parent Guide. If they do not participate, though, we have designed the book so that, if you are willing to work hard, you can use it on your own. If you are seeing a therapist, he or she also can help you to complete this program. In addition, you may currently be taking medication. However, medication does not substitute for a well-planned, systematic approach, such as the one presented in this book. With or without medication, this book can help you!

INTRODUCING SALLY SAMPLE

To help you with your task, we have created a cartoon character named "Sally Sample." Sally Sample has trichotillomania, and, like you, she is going to try this program. She will follow the instructions and complete the forms in each chapter, just as you will. After you see how she completes each form, write your own responses on the blank forms that you will find in the Appendix section of this book. We hope you will find that reading about her progress is interesting and useful.

Without further delay, let us now introduce Sally Sample:

Hi, I'm Sally, I am 14 years old and I am a freshman in high school. I have brown curly hair and brown eyes. I like horseback riding and cooking. I have a problem called trichotillomania, which means that I pull out my hair. I really wish that I could stop pulling out my hair so much. It's an embarrassing thing to do and it makes me look weird.

I remember the first time that I pulled my hair. I was 11 years old. I was doing my homework and feeling "antsy," but I knew I had to get it done. My head was leaning against my hand, and I started fiddling around with some strands of hair that were behind my left ear. Before I knew it, I had pulled out a few hairs.

In a way, the tingling feeling felt kind of good. In addition, pulling gave me something to do with my hands. By the time I had finished my homework, I had pulled out several more hairs. I threw them in the trash and didn't think any more about what I had done. But the next night, while I was watching TV, I started touching that same area behind my ear and before I knew it, I had pulled several more hairs from that spot. Over the next few weeks I found that I was playing with (and sometimes pulling out) hair from that same spot over and over again.

One day, I was brushing my hair and I noticed that there was a bald spot where I had been pulling. This really upset me, so I stopped pulling hair from that area. I pulled from behind the other ear instead, but unfortunately I just ended up creating a new bald spot. I also found myself starting to pull my eyelashes at times. I tried to stop pulling, but every time I bent my elbow it seemed like my hand automatically pulled my hair.

For a long time I kept my hair pulling a secret. I wore my hair in different styles or wore make up to hide the damage I had done.

I really tried to control my pulling. At one point, I was able to stop for a number of days. Slowly, new hair began to grow in. But this created a different problem, because when I touched the new growth, the prickly new hair felt so weird that I often pulled it out again!

One day I had just washed my hair and was going to my room when my mom saw my wet head. She gasped and said, "What on earth happened to your hair?" I couldn't hide the truth, so I told her everything, crying all the while. She told my dad and at first he got really angry. But after we talked about it, my parents calmed down and said that they would try to help by reminding me to stop pulling if they saw that my hand was near my head.

I know that my parents were just trying to help, but after that things got even worse! They would yell at me to stop pulling my hair every time I touched my head, even when I was only touching or scratching it. After a while I began to feel that they were trying to "catch" me pulling, and I began avoiding them. Since I almost always pull when I am alone, every time I would go to my room, my parents would accuse me of going there to pull my hair. I hate to admit it, but sometimes it was true. This constant tension made me want to avoid them even more. I found myself spending more and more time in my room, and more and more time pulling. I even started pulling in other parts of the house besides my bedroom.

Over the past three years I have tried to stop pulling many times. Occasionally, when I try really hard, I can resist pulling for a while. I even stopped for an entire summer one year, and my hair grew back. But once school started, I ended up pulling again, and undid all of my progress! I saw a therapist for a while, but it did not really help me decrease my pulling. My struggle with trich has been very frustrating for both my parents and me, but we have never given up the hope that I could find help. When I heard about this book, I decided to read it and see if it could help me control my hair pulling. As I go through each step, I will let you know how I am doing. I have a strong feeling that we will both make good progress!

In addition to Sally, the book also includes the image of a nine piece "Tricking Trich Puzzle" for you to "solve." Managing trich is like solving a puzzle: there are many pieces and, in the end, they all fit together to give you the "big picture"! We will show you a new piece of the puzzle at the beginning of each chapter, and at the end of the chapter we will show you how that new piece "fits into" the overall picture. When you finish Chapter 9, you will have "solved" the puzzle!

We know that working on this program will take time and effort, but with the help of Sally Sample and the "Tricking Trich Puzzle," we are confident that you will meet the challenge. So let's get started!

THE STEPS IN THIS BOOK

By reading this book you will learn:

- How to identify the features of **your unique hair pulling behavior** (Chapter 2);
- **Why** you pull your hair (Chapter 3);
- **Strategies** that will help you, and a plan for using them (Chapters 3-5);
- How to stay **motivated** (Chapter 6);
- How to put your plan into **action** (Chapter 7); and
- How to **stay on track** over the long run (Chapter 8).

SUMMARY

In this first chapter you learned that many people of all ages, male and female, struggle with the hair pulling problem called trichotillomania. You also met Sally, an imaginary girl who also has trich. She will "go first" in a lot of the things that we will be asking you to do. We think you will enjoy reading about her progress.

In the next chapter, you will begin gathering information on things that make your problem unique to you. You will need this information in order to develop **your** plan to trick trich!

In the meantime, re-member the "Trick-ing Trich Puzzle" you read about a few pages ago? Well, by reading this chapter and by **learning more about trich,** you have earned the **first piece of the puzzle!**

CHAPTER 2

GATHERING INFORMATION ABOUT YOUR "HABIT"

INTRODUCTION

In Chapter One, we hope you learned some new information about trich and about how this program works. In this chapter, we would like you to fill out a checklist so that you can learn more about the details of your unique hair pulling problem. Gathering this information will give you the second piece of the Tricking Trich Puzzle!

WHY YOU SHOULD BECOME A TRICH EXPERT

The best way to begin to solve your hair pulling problem is to learn about your unique hair pulling problem. This means being aware of when, where, and why you pull.

THE "INFORMATION ABOUT MY PULLING" CHECK-LIST

On the next several pages is a l-o-n-g checklist, called the *Information About My Pulling Checklist,* which will ask you a lot of questions about your hair pulling behavior. But before we ask you to work on it, we will have Sally Sample complete hers. Let's see what she has to say!

Hello again, it's me, Sally Sample. I am supposed to fill out this checklist now. I don't really want to, because thinking (much less writing) about trich really bothers me. But I am determined to get in control of this stupid problem that makes me feel so ashamed and frustrated. I want to be able to wear my hair any way I want to, to go swimming if I feel like it, and to go to school without worrying about people noticing my bald spots. So, if filling out the the checklist will help me "Trick Trich," I guess I'll do it. Here goes!

INFORMATION ABOUT MY PULLING CHECKLIST

1. Some people pull from a number of places on their bodies. Where on your body do you pull from?

I pull from my:

_x_	Head	_x_	Eyelashes
___	Eyebrows	___	Arms
___	Pubic Area	___	Underarms
___	Legs	___	Other _____

2. Some people pull mostly when they are in their own homes. Other people pull mostly outside of their homes. Still others pull equal amounts in and outside of the house.

I usually pull when I am:

In my house:

___	Living room
___	Dining room
_x_	Family room
___	Rec room
___	Kitchen
_x_	Bathroom
_x_	Bedroom
___	Other _____

Outside of my house:

___	Classroom
___	Library
___	Movie Theater
___	Car
___	Other _____

3. Many people pull with the help of some tool. Which, if any, of these do you use when you pull?

When I pull I sometimes use:

_x_ Mirror
___ Tweezers

4. Many people find that they pull while they are doing certain activities. Which of the following are likely to "trigger" hair pulling?

Doing my school work:

_x_ Desk/computer work
_x_ Studying/reading
___ Taking tests
___ Other _____

Transitions/making decisions:

___ Waking up in the morning
___ Deciding what to wear
_x_ Going to sleep
___ Other _____

Other:

_x_ Looking in the mirror
_x_ Leaning head on hand
___ Putting on make-up
___ Grooming (brushing hair, washing face, etc)

When my hands are not busy:

_x_ Talking on the phone
_x_ Lying in bed
___ Riding in the car
___ At the movies
_x_ Watching TV
___ Walking
___ Other _____

5.   Some people find that they pull when they experience certain emotions or internal states. What feelings are you having when you pull?

I pull when I feel:

___ Sad
_x_ Worried or Afraid
___ Bored
_x_ Angry with others
___ Angry with myself
_x_ Frustrated

_x_ Unsure about what to do
___ Excited
___ Happy
___ Hungry
___ Tired
___ Other _____

6. Some kids mistakenly think (or hope) that something "magical" will happen when they pull.

I pull for these superstitious reasons:

_x_ Revenge   ___ Luck
___ Getting rid of something bad   ___ Other _____

7. Many people find that certain characteristics about certain hairs really bother them or are interesting to see or touch, so they might pull out those hairs. Sometimes people are also bothered by certain results of the hair pulling, so they may pull more hair in order to "even out" or "correct" the "mistake."

I pull when I:

_x_ See out of place hairs   _x_ Touch sharp hairs
___ See uneven growth   _x_ Touch short hairs
___ See dark/light hairs   _x_ Touch thick hairs
___ Other _____

8. Many people find that they have certain sensations when they pull.

When I pull:

_x_ It feels good
___ It hurts
_x_ It feels tingly/interesting
_x_ I like the way it feels when I bite or play with the follicle/hair.
___ Other (Specify) _____

9. Some people will NOT pull in front of certain people, while others will pull in front of anyone.

I do NOT pull my hair in front of:

___ My parents   _x_ My classmates

___ My brother(s)   _x_ My teacher

___ My sister(s)   _x_ Strangers

_x_ My friends   ___ Other _____

10. People do very different things with the hair once it has been pulled.

After I pull hair out I:

_x_ Play with it   ___ Throw it out

___ Bite it   ___ Hide it

___ Swallow it*   ___ Leave it in a pile

___ Flush it down the toilet   ___ Other _____

(*Note: If you eat or swallow the hair, it can create serious health problems. Therefore it is very important that you tell your parents and see your doctor.)

11. Is there anything else about your hair pulling problem that was not asked? If so, make a note of it below. Remember that you want to find out as much as possible about your pattern of behavior so that you can come up with a really good plan!

Other features about my pulling:

_____

Whew, I'm done!   Once I got started filling out the list, I noticed that there was a pattern to my pulling. For instance, I saw that I tended to pull when I was studying in my room or talking on the phone in the family room or kitchen. A few days after I filled out the checklist, I noticed that I was pulling in front of the mirror in the bathroom, too, so I added that to the list as well. I can't believe I actually forgot about that the first time I worked on the list! Anyway, I did learn a lot about my problem from doing the list, and I think that you will, too.

☞☞☞   Now that you have read Sally's checklist and comments, it is your turn to complete your *Information About My Pulling Checklist*. You will find it in the Appendix on page A-151. You do not need to show it to anyone. In fact, if you want to, you can remove it from this book and put it in a private place. You will be referring back to this information later on in the book, so work on it carefully! Go ahead, you might find it kind of interesting!

AFTER COMPLETING YOUR CHECKLIST

Have you completed your *Information Checklist*? We hope that the answer is "yes," and that filling it in has helped you become more aware of your pulling patterns. But you know what? You still don't know **everything**. There may still be times when you pull your hair without being aware of what led to your pulling. Just because you have finished the checklist once does not mean that you are done! For the next week or so, whenever you realize that you have just pulled a hair, think about what was happening and where you were. Then, as soon as possible, be sure to check those items off on your *Checklist*. You are now on your way to becoming an expert about trich and your unique situation!

SUMMARY

In this chapter you worked on your *Information About My Pulling Checklist*, which helped you figure out when, why, where, and how you pull. Now that you have completed the checklist, you have earned the **second piece of the Tricking Trich Puzzle**. Over the next week or so, review and modify your checklist as needed. You may be surprised at what you notice about your hair pulling behavior! In the next chapter you will learn why people with trich pull their hair, and what techniques they (and you) can use to gain better control over trichotillomania!

CHAPTER 3

LEARNING ABOUT STRATEGIES

INTRODUCTION

In Chapter 2, you began to gather information about your hair pulling problem, including where, when, and how you pull; in other words, you identified your **trigger situations** and the **unique features of your hair pulling problem**. You looked at the *Information Checklist* and marked those items that apply to you. You then paid close attention to your pulling behavior and added new bits of information to your checklist as you noticed them. This information gave you the second piece of the Tricking Trich Puzzle.

In this chapter you will learn about why people pull their hair. You will also learn about some **strategies** that you can use **instead of pulling**.

WHY DO PEOPLE PULL THEIR HAIR?

1) Some people have a strong need to **fiddle** and/or **nibble**. Pulling hair and fiddling with it keeps their hands busy; nibbling, biting, or eating the hair keeps their mouths busy.

2) Some people pull their hair because they like the **sensation** they get from stimulating the scalp and/or skin. Others pull when they feel **physically uncomfortable**. Pulling hair seems to help them feel better.

3) Many people find that they pull their hair automatically, without even thinking about it. Other people find that even if they are aware, they just can't seem to keep their **hands** away from their hair. Their hands seem to have a "mind of their own."

4) Some people find that they pull in certain rooms or places. There seems to be something about those settings, or **environments**, that "trigger" pulling.

5) For some people, certain **emotions** create tension. Hair pulling seems to relieve the tension for the moment.

6) Many people are **"perfectionistic."** They become frustrated with hair that is not perfect. In addition, their imperfect efforts at controlling hair pulling can also lead to frustration. For these people, frustration or disappointment caused by perfectionism increases hair pulling.

Do any of these six problems sound familiar to you? Here is more information about them and some strategies that you can use to decrease pulling in each problem area:

IF YOU NEED TO KEEP YOUR HANDS OR MOUTH BUSY:

INSTEAD OF PULLING, FIDDLE WITH "HAND AND MOUTH ALTERNATIVES"

If you have trichotillomania, then it is very likely that you are a **fiddler,** and that you need to keep your hands and/or mouth busy most of the time. For you, situations that **trigger** pulling might include times when your body is "bored" and needs something to do. Sitting in school, watching TV, and talking on the phone are examples of situations where your hands or mouth might need something to do. However, these trigger situations do **not** necessarily have to result in pulling. **If you keep your hands and mouth busy with something really interesting before you get the urge to pull, then you will be much less likely to pull your hair.**

"Alternatives" are what we call the things that you can fiddle with instead of pulling. Playing with a **Koosh Ball, Silly Putty,** or other **fun-to-touch toys**, or fiddling around with **knotted lengths of dental floss,** are examples of **"hand alternatives."**

If you tend to nibble or chew the hair or bite the roots, you can **chew gum or suck on hard candy** instead. Some kids like to nibble on pieces of raw spaghetti. They like the way it "crunches"! These are examples of **"mouth alternatives."**

What other hand or mouth alternatives can you think of to fiddle with?

IF VARIOUS PARTS OF YOUR BODY NEED EXTRA ATTENTION:

INSTEAD OF PULLING, GIVE YOUR BODY THE ATTENTION IT NEEDS

For some people, the twinge they get as their hair is pulled from their scalp or skin feels kind of good. If this is the case with you, then **your skin and scalp may need to be scratched or otherwise stimulated** on a regular basis. In other words, those parts of your body may need a lot of special attention, which is also known as **sensory input** or **sensory stimulation**.

For other people, itchy or dry scalp or skin makes them scratch their scalp. Touching and scratching the scalp can then lead to hair pulling. For still others, the sensation that their skin tingles, burns, or, as some people put it, "glows," leads to touching the scalp and pulling. Often, pulling itself irritates the skin and leads to even more pulling. This creates a "vicious cycle" of pulling, skin irritation, and more pulling.

Do areas of your skin or scalp tend to bother you in these or similar ways? Does the tingly feeling of pulling feel good to you? If so, then you will need to give the areas where you pull **sensory input in the form of extra stimulation, attention, and pampering. Brushing or combing your hair more often, using lotions and bath oils, and/or using loofah sponges** regularly will soothe, soften, or stimulate your skin. **Once your skin is softer and less irritated, you will have fewer reasons to touch or scratch it, and therefore you will be less likely to pull.**

One twelve year old girl we know liked the feeling of scratching her scalp. Unfortunately, once she started scratching she often began to pull her hair. She decided to try spending about two minutes **combing conditioner through her hair when she was in the shower.** That strategy satisfied her need to scratch her scalp, and helped her decrease hair pulling .

Another way for you to take care of your body's needs is to **notice the sensations** you are having **inside** your body as well as on your skin and scalp. Like some kids, you may tend to pull when you are **tired, hungry, or restless.** If being **hungry** is a trigger situation for you, then when you notice that you are hungry you can use the obvious strategy of **having a snack**. If you are feeling restless and realize it, then you can **take a walk** instead of pulling your hair. The trick is to **train yourself to notice when you are hungry, restless, or otherwise physically uncomfortable, and then to do something constructive to help yourself feel better before you start pulling.**

One ten year old boy usually pulled his hair while doing homework after school. As he thought about when he pulled, he noticed that he was hungry and restless during that time of the day. He began to **eat a snack** and **ride his bicycle** for a little while every day before starting his homework. By taking care of his body's needs, he was better able to control his pulling.

What other ways of giving your body special attention can you think of?

IF YOUR HANDS "HAVE A MIND OF THEIR OWN":

FIND WAYS TO MAKE IT HARD TO PULL

As we already mentioned in Chapter 1, when it comes to hair pulling, it may sometimes feel like your hands "have a mind of their own." Therefore, you will need to become more **aware** of when your hands are reaching for your head or touching your hair. You will also need to find ways to interfere with or interrupt pulling once your fingers start to "search." You can do this by learning and using strategies that will make it **harder** for your fingers to grasp or successfully pull your hair. Here are some things that you can do to increase your awareness and interfere with pulling by making it **hard** to pull:

There are several strategies that you can use to interfere with pulling. For instance, wearing **"rubber fingertips"** on your thumbs and/or fingers, or wearing **scarves** or **hats** on your head **can be very helpful in stopping your hand from automatically getting to its "target."**

Several girls we know tend to pull their hair when they are trying to get to sleep at night. They have found that they can create a barrier by wearing **lightweight cotton gloves tied at the wrists with pretty ribbons.** Other young people have used **Band-Aids** on their thumbs and/or fingertips to help them keep their hands away from their hair.

Another way to make it hard to pull is by doing something to your hair that makes it more difficult to grasp. For instance, you may find that you do not tend to pull your hair if it is **wet** or **greasy.** If so, try putting **conditioner** in your hair (and rinsing it out later), **taking a quick shower/shampoo**, or just **spraying your hair with water.** This might make it just hard enough to grasp the hair so that you can **delay** pulling for a few minutes. In the meantime, you may be able to distract yourself by **getting involved in other activities (including using your alternatives) long enough to lose the urge to pull.**

You might also make it hard to pull your hair by **cutting your hair short, growing it long, or wearing it in a tight ponytail.** Any hairstyle that makes your hair less interesting or more difficult to pull will help you decrease pulling.

You can also interfere with hair pulling behavior by **changing your position when you are sitting or lying down.** For instance, if you pull hair from your head, you may tend to sit with your right elbow bent and your head resting against your hand. **By sitting in a different position you can break the automatic hair pulling cycle.**

One girl practiced sitting **on the middle of the couch instead of at the end.** That way she avoided resting her bent elbow on the arm of the couch. A boy we know started wearing an **athletic elastic band** around his elbow so that he would not easily be able to bend his arm. In both cases, since the elbows were not easily bent, these people were less likely to pull.

What else can you think of to make it hard to pull?

IF SOMETHING IN YOUR EVIRONMENT TRIGGERS PULLING:

INSTEAD OF PULLING, CHANGE YOUR ENVIRONMENT

When you filled out your *Information Checklist*, did you note that you tend to pull when you are in certain rooms of your house? That means that just being in those rooms may "trigger" pulling behavior. Once you are aware of the **locations** that trigger pulling, you can make a change in those environments. This will help you decrease pulling.

> One fifteen year old girl pulled her hair whenever she went into a certain bathroom, even if she just went in to wash her hands. She would automatically look in the mirror, start touching her hair, and then (you guessed it!), she would start pulling. She decided to try using another bathroom rather than the one she usually used. The "new" bathroom created a different environment, which helped her gain better control of her pulling.

However, you can't always avoid certain rooms. It would be impossible, for instance, for you to avoid your bedroom. So you also need to be able to find ways to change things **within** "trigger" rooms. Here are some suggestions for changes that you can make in rooms where you tend to pull:

- If you use a mirror when you pull, and the room has a mirror (for instance, in your bedroom or bathroom), **cover the mirror.** If you cannot cover the mirror, forbid yourself to stand closer than an arm's length away from it.

- Leave the doors open in rooms where you tend to pull unless you absolutely need privacy.

- Get **rid** of (or have your parents hide) certain "tools of destruction" that are in your environment (like tweezers, for instance.) If you tweeze your eyebrows, ask someone else to tweeze them for you.

- **Rearrange the furniture** in the room, or sit in a different seat when you are in that room.

- Put **"visual cues/reminders"** in the room to remind yourself that you are entering a **"danger zone."** Some visual reminders might be **notes of encouragement (such as, "Don't Pull!" or "Use Your Strategies!") or a picture of a stop sign on the door or mirror.** These visual cues should remind you to grab hold of and use your strategies or to leave that room as soon as possible.

By **setting up or changing your environment before you have an urge to pull your hair, you help can yourself to trick trich!** One teenage girl tended to pull her hair when she was watching television in the family room. When she sat in a certain chair, she would automatically turn on the light, and reach for the tweezers and mirror that she kept nearby. With increased awareness, she realized that she needed to change her environment. She started **sitting in a different chair**, and asked her parents to **hide the mirror and tweezers**. She made sure that she had plenty of alternatives to "play" with close at hand (she especially liked Koosh Balls). Changing her environment (along with fiddling with her alternatives) helped her greatly increase her control over TTM.

What other ways can you think of to change your environment?

IF CERTAIN EMOTIONS LEAD YOU TO PULL YOUR HAIR:

INSTEAD OF PULLING, DEAL WITH YOUR EMOTIONS IN A BETTER WAY

Some people who pull their hair do so when they are feeling certain **emotions,** such as excitement, anger, boredom, or frustration. If this sometimes happens to you, it is very important (for your general well being as well as to help you control TTM) for you to **find better ways to deal with those feelings**. For instance, if you pull when you feel frustrated or angry, you can tell yourself that you will only hurt yourself twice when you pull your hair in those situations: first, by doing damage to your hair, and second, by not solving the problem! Learning problem-solving skills such as **talking things over, writing down how you feel, or doing yoga or exercising when your body is tense are much better ways to cope with strong emotions.**

Do you pull when you are bored, making a decision, or feeling impatient? If so, an activity such as **doodling** or using one of your **fiddling alternatives** should help. Strategies for dealing with **stress** created by emotional trigger situations might include **getting some physical exercise, learning relaxation exercises, brushing your hair, or hopping in the shower.**

When one twelve year old girl we know was angry with her parents, she would go to her room and pull her hair. This relieved the tension that she was feeling at the moment, and also made her feel like she was "getting back" at her parents. However, she really wanted to gain control over trich because it caused her so much embarrassment. With her therapist's help, she and her parents found that talking things over when there was a problem was a better way to solve their differences. This girl was proud of herself for learning how to work things out with her parents, and she was equally proud that she was able to decrease her hair pulling behavior!

Can you think of some more constructive ways to manage your emotions?

IF YOU ARE PERFECTIONISTIC:

INSTEAD OF PULLING, BE MORE FLEXIBLE

Some people who have trich tend to pull their hair because of **perfectionistic thoughts and attitudes**. "Perfectionism" is when people have **unrealistic standards or think that things have to be one certain way.**

BEING PERFECTIONISTIC ABOUT YOUR <u>HAIR:</u>

Perfectionistic thoughts about your hair can increase pulling. For instance, does it bother you that some of your hairs are thinner, thicker, or curlier than others? If so, you might pull those hairs out. Is it unacceptable to you when new hair growth is uneven, differs in color or texture from the rest of your hair, or feels prickly? If that is the case, you might tend to pull out new hair growth because it feels or looks different from the rest of your hair, or simply because the new growth is not even. These are all examples of perfectionistic thinking, and this kind of unrealistic thinking can definitely trigger pulling behavior.

Here are some reasons why expecting your hair to be exactly even in length, color or texture is so unrealistic: First, there is **natural variety** of color and texture in normal, healthy hair. In addition, some people are born with light hair that turns darker over time. Others may have curly hair that straightens out as they get older. Being able to tolerate natural variations in the color or texture of your hair is extremely important if you are to manage TTM.

Second, hair grows in at different rates on different parts of the head and body, and at different rates during the various seasons of the year. Therefore, the new hair will **not** grow in evenly at first. However, **if you are able to resist the urge to pull, eventually most or all of your hair will grow in fully and evenly.**

Third, most hair is stubby or prickly when it first grows in after having been pulled. If you pull out the new growth, the next hair will initially grow in prickly as well. But if you are able to leave the new growth alone, after a few weeks it will become soft to the touch.

Finally, hair has a **natural life span**. Each individual hair grows in, stays for a period of time, and eventually falls out. At that time a new hair grows in to take its place. When hair is allowed to go through its natural life span, new growth is generally similar in appearance to the hair it has replaced. However, when a hair has been pulled out repeatedly, the root (also known as the follicle) becomes temporarily damaged, and the new growth may look quite different from the rest of your hair. It may grow in thick, very thin, crooked, curly, or a different color. After growing in for a few months, its appearance may improve somewhat. Eventually, it will finish its life cycle. If it has not been pulled out, its root has had a chance to "rest," and the **next** hair that grows in should look very much like the rest of your hair.

Pulling out the initial regrowth because the hairs look different will **not** "fix" them. Pulling those hairs only repeats the growth of the hairs you do not like. If you pull out a crooked hair, for instance, it will be replaced by another crooked hair! So allowing time for the hair to grow back **twice** is really important. Being able to put up with the unusual hairs that grow in first will help the second growth to come back just like the rest of your hair.

BEING PERFECTIONISTIC ABOUT YOUR <u>BEHAVIOR</u>

Perfectionistic thinking about your efforts to stop pulling can actually <u>increase</u> pulling. How many times have you said you yourself, "Today I am going to stop pulling for good"? Well, that is **perfectionistic thinking.** If you have that expectation, then the moment you pull even one hair, you might feel that you have broken your agreement with yourself. When this happens, kids sometimes go on pulling "binges," figuring that since they have failed, they might as well just keep on pulling.

Because perfectionistic thinking can lead to pulling, the best attitude for you to have regarding TTM is for your thinking to be **realistic and flexible**. An example of flexible thinking is **telling yourself that you will do the best that you can today.** Then if you do pull, you think about **what you might do differently the next time**. In the long run, that attitude is what you will need to trick trich!

We know a boy who could be in good control for weeks at a time. However, once he pulled one or two hairs, he would be so disappointed in himself that he would keep on pulling until he had done major damage. Finally, **he learned to accept that he would occasionally "slip."** When he pulled out some hair, instead of giving up, he started saying things like, **"I'll just do the best I can,"** and **"I know that I can keep this problem small and get back on track."** He also reminded himself that **mistakes are learning opportunities.** When he would have a "bad" day, he would tell himself that he had had many successes but that no one is perfect. Then he would think about **what he would do differently** the next time that trigger situation came up. In other words, he started thinking **in realistic and flexible ways**. This helped him **do good problem solving**. As you can imagine, he began to make excellent progress!

What else can you say to yourself so that you will not engage in perfectionistic thinking?

SO THAT'S WHY I PULL!

We expect that many of the situations that we have just described look familiar to you. If so, then you now know why you pull in some situations but not in others. Pretty interesting, isn't it? We will refer back to these reasons for pulling later on in the book, so you may want to review this chapter from time to time. Knowing why you pull is an important step in learning how to **effectively manage** trich.

INTRODUCING THE STRATEGIES LIST

Once you figure out **why** you pull, you can then come up with strategies to help yourself **not** pull. On the next few pages you will find a lot of strategies listed, which you can use to decrease pulling. These strategies address each of the six reasons why people pull: 1) the need to fiddle, 2) sensory needs, 3) hands have a mind of their own, 4) environmental triggers, 5) emotional triggers, 6) perfectionism.

☞☞☞ **Circle, highlight,** or **underline** strategies in each section of the list that you already use or that you think you might want to try. Feel free to add your own ideas to each list. Remember, anything goes, so be creative!

COMPREHENSIVE STRATEGIES LIST

1. FIDDLE WITH HAND AND/OR MOUTH ALTERNATIVES

Koosh Ball

Pot scrubber

Mushroom or potato brush

Silly Putty

Belly ball

Rub sand paper

File/polish nails

Brush the family pet

Draw/paint

Modeling clay

Chew gum

Bite pieces of raw spaghetti

Suck on hard candy

Chew on a toothpick

Eat sesame or poppy seeds

Smooth stone

Vegetable brush

Worry beads

Rub a blanket

Rub knotted dental floss

Knitting or needlepoint

Bead jewelry

Color in a coloring book

String art

Paper cut-out collage

Chew on a straw

Floss your teeth

Eat sunflower seeds

Eat gummy bears

Your ideas _Wire_____

2. MEET YOUR BODY'S <u>SENSORY</u> NEEDS

Use facial scrub/mask

Rub ice on face or head

Rub something smooth on your face

Get a manicure

Use a loofah sponge

Use bath oil

Brush your hair often

Floss your teeth

Use dandruff shampoo

Use hand cream

Use a massage brush

Use an anti-itch cream

Your ideas _____

3. INCREASE YOUR AWARENESS / MAKE IT <u>HARD</u> TO PULL YOUR HAIR

Wear Band-Aids on fingertips

Wear "rubber fingers"

Wear glasses

Keep your hair wet

Use an elbow brace

Change your hairstyle

Use a deep conditioner

Wear tape on fingertips

Wear a hat

Wear cotton gloves

Use a thumb brace

Get rid of your tweezers

Put petroleum jelly on your eyelids

Wear a bracelet with bells on it

Your ideas _____

4.   CHANGE YOUR <u>ENVIRONMENT</u>

Cover the mirror

Lower the lights

Place reminder notes around

Keep the door open

Sit on the floor

Remove the mirror

Sit in a different place

Avoid the room

Rearrange the furniture

Your ideas _____

5. DEAL WITH YOUR <u>EMOTIONS</u> IN A BETTER WAY

Talk about how you feel
Exercise
Take a shower or bath
Meditate
Do something fun
Learn to compromise

Go for a walk
Call a friend
Write your feelings down
Keep a journal
Take a break
Do relaxation exercises

Your ideas *Playing with pillow and reading, and screaming into pillow*

6. DON'T BE <u>PERFECTIONISTIC</u>

Look at your progress, not just the "slips."
Use the strategies that **are** working for you.
Think positively (I think I can. I think I can.)
Remember that pulling out hair will not "fix" it.
Expect that hair will grow back unevenly at first.

Try one step at a time, not all at once.
Try a new strategy every two weeks or so.
Practice being imperfect (and having that be o.k.)
Remind yourself that your hair will grow back imperfectly at first.

Your ideas _____

FIDDLING SHEEP

Once you know **why** you pull, you can choose different kinds of strategies that meet your needs. But the six kinds of strategies (**fiddle**, meet your **sensory** needs, make it **hard** to pull, change your **environment**, deal with your **emotions** in better ways, and avoid **perfectionistic** thinking) might be hard to remember. So we have come up with the following memory technique, known as a mnemonic device (pronounced "new-mon-ik"), to make it easier for you:

The first step is to imagine a very silly picture—that of a sheep playing a fiddle—in other words, a **"fiddling sheep."** Now we will explain how the image of a "fiddling sheep" will help you:

• First, let's look at the word **"Fiddling."** This word will remind you that you probably are a fiddler. If so, you need to keep your hands and mouth busy. Remember to use hand and mouth alternatives.

• Now take the letters **S-H-E-E-P** to help you remember the rest of the information:

S: stands for "Meet your **Sensory Needs**." Your skin and scalp may need scratching, soothing, rubbing, or other kinds of sensory stimulation, so remember to use strategies that give your skin sensory input.

H: stands for "Make it **Hard** to pull." Hair pulling may be an automatic behavior--you may do without thinking about it or in spite of your desire to stop yourself. In fact, it may feel at times as if your hands have a mind of their own. Therefore, you may need to use barriers or other strategies that will increase your awareness and that will make it hard to pull.

E: stands for "Change your **Environment**." You may tend to pull in certain rooms in your house or in certain other environments. Therefore, you may be able to reduce pulling by changing certain aspects of your environment.

E(m): stands for "Deal with your **Emotions** in better ways." You may pull when you are angry, bored, frustrated or excited. This will remind you that there are many self-calming and problem-solving strategies that you can use to deal with various emotions rather than pulling your hair.

P: stands for "Don't be **Perfectionistic**." Recognize when you are being perfectionistic and use self-talk strategies to keep your thinking flexible.

Now that you know what the words and letters **"Fiddling SHEEP"** stand for, you can use this mnemonic device to help you. Take a few minutes over the next few days to memorize what the "fiddling sheep" image represents, so that it will be easy for you to remember the different kinds of strategies that you can use.

Hello, again! While reading this chapter, I began to realize more and more things about my pulling behavior. I also read the strategies lists and started to think about some things that I could do to help myself. By using the "Fiddling SHEEP" idea I thought of several strategies that might help me. First, I found out that I definitely am a "fiddler"! So when I saw "Silly Putty" on the "Hands and Mouth Alternatives" list and remembered that I had enjoyed playing with it when I was younger, I circled it as an alternative that I will try. I might also try using Band-Aids or rubber fingers as barriers to help me keep my hands away from my hair. I need to think about changing my environment, too. I also know that I need to be flexible and not perfectionistic when I have a "slip." Boy, there is so much to think about! I guess I need a plan to help me organize myself. Maybe the next chapter will help me. See you there!

SUMMARY

In this important chapter you learned about six problems that can lead to pulling. In addition, you learned about the different kinds of strategies that you can use to handle those problems: **fiddle**, meet your **sensory** needs, make it **hard** to pull, change your **environment**, deal with your **emotions** in better ways, and don't be **perfectionistic**. You also found out about the phrase **"fiddling sheep,"** which will help you remember those different categories. This was a big and important chapter. Congratulations, you got through it and earned the **third piece of the Tricking Trich Puzzle!**

In the next chapter we will show you how to organize your trigger situations and possible strategies into a *Problem Solving Chart*.

CHAPTER 4

CREATING YOUR PROBLEM SOLVING CHART

INTRODUCTION

Let's review the work that you have done so far:

Chapter 1: You learned about trichotillomania and how managing it is like **solving a puzzle**--that there are many pieces, and that you will need to put all the pieces together in order to be successful.

Chapter 2: You used the *Information About My Pulling Checklist* to learn more about your unique pattern of pulling behavior.

Chapter 3: You learned about various reasons why people pull their hair. You also learned about different kinds of **strategies** that you can use to prevent or decrease pulling.

In this chapter you will make a *Problem Solving Chart,* which will help you choose **strategies to use in each of your specific trigger situations.** By the time you finish this chapter you will have gotten the fourth piece of the Tricking Trich Puzzle!

PUTTING THE PIECES TOGETHER

The *Problem Solving Chart,* which is on the next page (blank forms are on page A-155 in the Appendix), has several columns and rows. This form will be used for a couple of purposes.

The first purpose of the form is to help you be more aware of what your "trigger" situations are. Trigger situations are found by noticing **where** you are and **what** you are doing when you pull.

Across the top row are boxes where you can write down activities that you are involved in (like talking on the phone, studying, taking tests) where you notice that you pull your hair. Down the left side of the form are spaces where you can write up to four locations (for example, specific rooms in your house, the car, or your classroom) where you generally pull. The boxes where the locations and activities "come together" are your **trigger situations**. You might want to **highlight** those boxes.

For the next three or four days we would like you to write down how many hairs you pulled during each pulling episode. If you do not want to write down the numbers (or can't remember how many hairs you pulled), then just put a checkmark or "x." This might be embarrassing to do, but it is an important part of analyzing your hair pulling behavior. (When you are in school you can make little notes on the corner of a piece of notebook paper and transfer the information to your chart when you get home.) You can change the headings if you see that the chart does not include your main trigger locations or activities. Let's see how Sally filled in her chart:

PROBLEM SOLVING CHART

ACTIVITIES THAT TRIGGER PULLING →→→→→→→→→→→

LOCATIONS →→→	WATCHING TV	DOING HOMEWORK	GETTING READY FOR BED	TALKING ON THE PHONE
FAMILY ROOM	10, 15, 13, 20			8 12
BATHROOM			13, 8, X	
BEDROOM	21, 14, 20, 9, 8, 7, X	24, X, 14, 27, 11, 2, 3, 21, 16	13, 15, 11	5 9 11

Each number shows how many hairs Sally pulled during each pulling episode. She put an "X" when she did not remember how many hairs she pulled, but she did know that she pulled some hairs. Notice that Sally did the most pulling when she was in her bedroom--it is her worst "trigger" location.

Hi, this is Sally Sample again. As you can see, I wrote down the places and activities that create trigger situations for me. Then for about four days I kept track of how often I pulled when I was in those trigger situations. I even tried to down how many hairs I pulled, which was really hard for me to do because I was so embarrassed. But at the end of the four days I saw a lot of things that were interesting to me. For instance, I never realized what a big trigger being in my room was! I also noticed that getting ready for bed was a problem for me, both in the bathroom and in my bedroom. After four days I was ready to write up my chart again, this time putting strategy ideas in the "Trigger Situation" boxes. I thought about when, where, and why I pulled in each situation. Then I went over the Strategies List in Chapter Two and found strategies in various categories that I thought might help me. I came up with quite a few ideas!

PROBLEM SOLVING CHART

ACTIVITIES
↓   ↓   ↓   ↓

LOCATIONS ↓ ↓ ↓	Watching TV
Family Room	TRIGGER SITUATION (10, 15, 13, 20 hairs pulled)

As you can see, there is a shaded box which shows where the activities (for instance, "Watching TV") and the location ("Family Room," for example) "come together." Sally added up the numbers and saw that she had pulled almost 60 hairs in that trigger situation in the previous four days! She now realizes that she will need to use some strategies in that situation. At this point the chart can be used for its **second** purpose. Using a **new** *Problem Solving Chart* form, Sally will rewrite the locations and activities across the top row and left side column of her form. Then, in the trigger situation boxes, she will write down the strategies that she plans to use, starting with when she is watching TV in the family room. Sally's choices of strategies will be based on her unique needs.

What will some of those strategies be? Well, remember what Sally wrote about her pulling behavior when she introduced herself in Chapters 1 and 2? Using that information, let's see which strategies she will try when she is watching TV in the family room. When Sally thinks about it, she realizes that in that situation: 1) her hands get restless; 2) she pulls automatically -- her hands seem to have a mind of their own; and 3) she always sits in the same position in the same chair when she pulls. Let's see how Sally uses this information to choose her strategies:

1) FIDDLE WITH HAND AND MOUTH ALTERNATIVES

Sally now knows that she needs to keep her hands busy when she is watching TV in the family room. Therefore, every time Sally is in that trigger situation, she will plan to have something to "play with" so that she will be less likely to pull her hair.

Her alternatives, or "toys," will help keep her hands busy when she is watching TV. These supplies should be within arm's reach so that Sally will not have to get up to look for them in order to use them.

Sally looked back at her *Strategies List* and saw that **Silly Putty** was listed in the "fiddling" section. Remembering that when she was younger she had enjoyed playing with Silly Putty, she decided to give it a try it as a strategy that she could use to keep her hands busy. She wrote "Silly Putty" in the appropriate box in her *Problem Solving Chart.* Sally will plan to fiddle with Silly Putty in that trigger situation, **whether or not she has the urge to pull**. She knows that she is someone who needs to keep her hands busy, so she will meet that need by **fiddling with Silly Putty instead of fiddling with and pulling out her hair.**

Sally also wrote (F) on her chart to remind her that this strategy meets her need to fiddle. Here is what her chart is beginning to look like:

PROBLEM SOLVING CHART

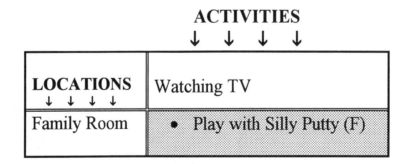

(F) =Fiddle with Hand and/or Mouth Alternatives

2) MAKE IT HARD TO PULL

In order to make it hard to pull for her to pull her hair, first Sally will need to **notice** when her hand is reaching for her head. Next, she will need to find a way to **prevent** her fingers from successfully grasping and pulling her hair. This is best done by using strategies that create **"barriers"** or that otherwise **interfere** with pulling behavior.

Sally has chosen to wear **rubber fingers** on her thumbs while she watches TV in the family room. The rubber fingers will help her in a few different ways. First, by increasing her awareness, they are good reminders for her not to play with her hair. Second, the rubber fingers have little nubs on them, which makes them fun to touch and fiddle with. But most important, because they are a **barrier** between her fingers and her hair, when she wears them it is almost impossible for Sally to pull her hair. Here is how her chart looks with the addition of this strategy:

PROBLEM SOLVING CHART

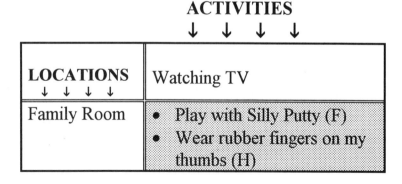

ACTIVITIES
↓ ↓ ↓ ↓

LOCATIONS ↓ ↓ ↓ ↓	Watching TV
Family Room	• Play with Silly Putty (F) • Wear rubber fingers on my thumbs (H)

(F) = **Fiddle** with Hand and/or Mouth Alternatives
(H) = Make it **hard** to pull your hair

3) CHANGE YOUR ENVIRONMENT

Sally has "her" seat in the family room. This is the place where she is most comfortable, and the place where she is most likely to pull her hair. She has decided to **change her environment** by sitting in a different seat (or on the floor) for several weeks to see if this helps in her efforts to stop pulling. This is what Sally's chart looks like now:

PROBLEM SOLVING CHART

ACTIVITIES
↓   ↓   ↓   ↓

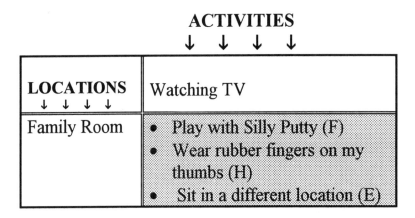

LOCATIONS ↓ ↓ ↓ ↓	Watching TV
Family Room	• Play with Silly Putty (F) • Wear rubber fingers on my thumbs (H) • Sit in a different location (E)

(F) = **Fiddle** with Hand and/or Mouth Alternatives
(H) = Make it **hard** to pull your hair
(E) = Change your **environment**

There are probably many more strategies that Sally could choose to help her manage her pulling when she is watching TV in the family room. However, **if she uses these three strategies every day**, she has an excellent chance of **decreasing** or even **eliminating her pulling** in that situation!

Hello, it's Sally again. I am now going to take some time now to finish my Problem Solving Chart. As you might remember, my trigger situations include not only watching TV, but also doing homework, getting ready for bed, and talking on the phone. I will use each of these activities as the headings for my columns. I will also add "bathroom" and "bedroom" sections to the chart, since I also pull in those rooms. I am excited about getting things going so that I can begin to trick trich!

Now look at the next page to see the completed *Problem Solving Chart* that Sally Sample came up with. Sally noted that there were three rooms where she pulled and four main activities that triggered pulling. Notice that she decided to use a variety of different strategies in each trigger situation. She knows that there is no one "magic answer." A nice thing about this chart is that some boxes are blank. This is a reminder that she, like all kids with trich, does **not** pull in every location or situation!

PROBLEM SOLVING CHART

ACTIVITIES THAT TRIGGER PULLING

LOCATIONS	Watching TV	Doing Homework	Getting Ready for Bed	Talking on the Phone
Family Room	• Play with Silly Putty (F) • Wear rubber fingers on my thumbs (H) • Sit in a different chair (E)			• Make beaded earrings (F) • Wear my hair in a pony tail (H) • Put a reminder note on the phone (E)
Bathroom			• Wash my face with a textured sponge (E) • Cover the mirror (E)	
Bedroom	• Play with Koosh Ball (F) • Wear a hat (H) • Put a note on the TV (E)	• Play with mushroom brush (F) • Brush hair (E) • Wear Band-Aids on my fingers (H)	• Wear hand lotion with gloves (H) or • Wear Band-Aids at night when I go to sleep (H) • Try a new strategy (P)	• File or polish nails (F) • Wear Scotch tape on finger tips; put petroleum jelly on eyelids (H) • Take a deep breath and talk about what is bothering me (Em)

F = **Fiddle** with hand and /or mouth alternatives
S = Meet your body's **Sensory** needs
H = Make it **Hard** to pull your hair
E = Change your **Environment**
E(m) = Deal with your **Emotions** in a better way
P = Don't be **Perfectionistic**

☞☞☞ Now turn to the *Problem Solving Chart* in the Appendix on page A-155, and write your trigger activities across the top and your trigger locations down the left hand column. Where the activities and rooms "come together," highlight those boxes. These are your "trigger" situations. Begin by filling in one of the highlighted boxes by writing down some strategies that you might use in that situation. Then go on to another box. Start small and fill in the chart little by little so that you don't get overwhelmed. Use a pencil so that you can make changes as you go along. Eventually, you will have all the highlighted boxes filled it!

SUMMARY

In this chapter you were introduced to the *Problem Solving Chart*. You learned how to create your own chart by writing down activities and locations that trigger pulling. Then you learned how to complete your chart by writing **strategies** that will help you in those situations. You became aware of the importance of including a **variety** of different kinds of strategies in each trigger situation. Finally, you were reminded that you do not have to complete your *Problem Solving Chart* all at once but can work on it a little at a time. You now have the fourth piece of the **Tricking Trich Puzzle**. Turn the page and see how the puzzle looks so far!

CHAPTER 5

DEVELOPING YOUR PLAN

INTRODUCTION

In the last chapter you created your *Problem Solving Chart*. In this chapter we will show you how to use your *Problem Solving Chart* to develop a plan. You will do this by learning how to: **1) set up your environment** and **2) write a weekly chart.**

1) SETTING UP YOUR ENVIRONMENT

Now that you have come up with some strategies that you think will help you in trigger situations, you need to set up the rooms where you will be using those strategies. Review your *Problem Solving Chart*. What strategies do you plan to use in each room? What supplies will you need? Now write down the list of supplies that you will need, room by room. Note which ones you already have at home and which ones you will need to buy. Will your parents pay for them or will you buy them with your own money? Talk with your parents, and come up with an agreement about this.

Before you go shopping, put the supplies that you already have in several boxes or baskets that you have labeled by room, one basket for each trigger location. If your trigger situation is not at home you can put your supplies in your purse, in your backpack, or in a bag.

After you have put your supplies in the baskets, arrange for your parents to take you shopping for those you still need. You might not find everything in one shopping trip, but try to get enough items so that you will have a good selection of alternatives to start with. When you have your new supplies, add them to the appropriate box or basket.

Let's look at an example of one eleven-year-old boy. This boy pulled hair from the top of his head and bit off the follicles. One of his trigger situations was when he was in the den doing homework at the computer or working on his baseball card collection, especially when he was trying to decide which cards to sell, trade, or buy. Here is how he set up his environment:

After completing his *Information About My Pulling Checklist* and his *Problem Solving Chart*, the boy made his supply list, beginning with the den.   Recognizing that he was a **fiddler**, he wrote down "raw spaghetti, gum, and hard candy" as alternatives that would keep his mouth busy, and "Koosh Ball" for keeping his hands busy. Because he sometimes pulled without realizing it, he wrote down that he could wear a baseball cap as a barrier. In addition, the boy listed "sticky notes" as an **environmental** strategy that he could use. These notes, which he could stick on the computer screen and on his baseball card boxes, could give him words of encouragement such as, "Hands Down," "Keep Cap On," or "Play

With Koosh Ball!"

His supply list was ready and included what he already had and what he would need to get. Here is what it looked like:

Supplies for Den

Raw spaghetti   OK
Baseball cap   OK
Koosh Ball   Need to buy
Sticky notes   OK

A few days later, the boy finished writing his list by writing down the things that he would need in his other trigger situations. The boy then filled some boxes with the alternatives that he already had. Later that week, his parents took him shopping for the rest of his supplies. When he had made his purchases, he added them to his collection and put the boxes in the appropriate rooms. The box for the den contained some raw spaghetti, gum, a baseball cap, a Koosh Ball, and some sticky notes.

This boy was surprised that he was able to organize things so easily. But it was easy because he had prepared himself by completing his *Problem Solving Chart* before taking the next step. It will be easy for you, too!

Sally Sample also reviewed her *Problem Solving Chart* before she set up her environment. You may want to look back at Chapter 4 so that you can see how she chose her supplies. Look at the next page to see what she did:

Once I finished filling out my Problem Solving Chart, I was

ready to make a list of supplies that I would need. I knew that I would need a lot of supplies in my bedroom, because so many activities that I do in there are triggers for me -- watching TV, doing homework, getting ready for bed, and talking on the phone. Here is what I came up with:

1) Since I am a <u>fiddler</u> I put some "Hand and Mouth Alternatives" on my list: a Koosh Ball, a plastic mushroom brush, a nail file, and a few bottles of nail polish.

2) Because my scalp seems to likes getting <u>sensory stimula-tion</u>, I included a brush on the list.

3) To make it <u>hard</u> to pull, I will need to use some barriers. I listed wearing a hat and using rubber fingers while watching TV. I also included Band-Aids to wear on my thumbs while I am doing homework, and cotton gloves, which I can wear at night.

4) I listed "sticky notes" as an <u>environmental</u> strategy. That way I can write encouraging notes to myself and put them around my room.

When I was done, my supply list for my bedroom included: <u>a Koosh Ball, a plastic mushroom brush, a nail file, a brush, a hat, rubber fingers, Band-Aids, cotton gloves, and sticky notes.</u> I *found most of the items around the house, and put them in a box labeled "bedroom." Then I went through the same process for the bathroom and family room, which are my other trigger locations. When I was done, I wrote out a shopping list for the things I did not already have.*

That weekend my mom took me to the shopping mall, where I was able to get most of the rest of my supplies. I added them to my boxes and baskets, which I then put in the appropriate rooms.

Go ahead now and make a list of your supplies based on your *Problem Solving Chart.* Purchase the items that you need, and put them in boxes or baskets along with the supplies that you already have. Once you have collected your supplies, put them in your trigger rooms.

2) YOUR WEEKLY CHART

It is time to write your *Weekly Chart,* which will be your **most important aid** in this whole book! Your *Weekly Chart* will look very much like your *Problem Solving Chart,* except it will include days of the week so that you can keep track of how often you use your strategies. Although it covers a whole week, the chart should be checked off on a daily basis.

Writing up your *Weekly Chart* should be easy! You have already worked on your *Problem Solving Chart,* so all you have to do is transfer the information. Start with one room, and write down the activities that you do in that room that trigger pulling. Write down between two and four strategies that you will use in each of those situations, including their "fiddling sheep" initials. Be sure that you list a good variety of strategies! Do the same thing for two or three other rooms.

By the time you finish your *Weekly Chart* you will have three or four rooms/locations listed, along with trigger situations, as well as strategies that you can use in each. **The strategies should be used on a daily basis, whether or not you have the urge to pull!**

Before you actually write up your *Weekly Chart*, take a look at how Sally did hers:

Hi again. I used my Problem Solving chart to create my Weekly Chart. It was pretty easy to do. Here is how I set it up:

1) I started out by writing down "Family Room" in the left hand column.

2) Under "Family Room" I listed "watching TV," which is a trigger situation for me.

3) In the next column, across from "watching TV," I wrote down several strategies that I plan to try when I am watching TV in the family room.

4) I wrote the appropriate "fiddling sheep" initial next to each item and tried to choose a good variety of different kinds of strategies.

5) I did the same thing for the bathroom and bedroom.

6) I checked my baskets and boxes to make sure that I had the supplies that I needed.

I did not include all of my trigger rooms and situations, nor did I write down all of the strategies that I plan to use. I will start with a few things on my chart so that I won't get overwhelmed. As time goes on, I can make changes and additions. Here's how it came out:

SALLY'S WEEKLY CHART

Date Started

LOCATION/ACTIVITY	STRATEGY	S	M	T	W	T	F	S
Family Room								
• watching TV	Play with silly putty (F)							
	Wear rubber fingers (H)							
	Sit in a different chair (E)							
Bathroom	Wash face w/textured sponge (S)							
	Cover mirror (E)							
Bedroom								
• doing homework	Play with mushroom brush (F)							
	Brush hair (S)							
• getting ready for bed	Wear band aids on fingers (H)							
• talking on phone	Make beaded earrings (F)							
	Wear ponytail (H)							
	Use my "imperfect" strategies, even when I don't feel like it (P)							

F = **Fiddle**
S = Meet your **Sensory** needs
H = Make it **Hard** to pull
E = Change your **Environment**
E(m) =Deal with your **Emotions** in a better way
P = Don't be **Perfectionistic**

☞☞☞   Now that you have read Sally's *Weekly Chart*, please go ahead and work on your own chart. There are several copies of the form on page A-157. (For now, don't worry about the part of the chart that deals with "points." We'll be talking about that topic in the next few chapters!) We think that you will be pleased to see how well you do!

SUMMARY

In this chapter you learned how to **set up your environment** to help you prevent or reduce pulling. You did this by reviewing your *Problem Solving Chart,* and by using that information to choose strategies that you can use when you are in trigger situations. You collected your supplies, and put them in all the rooms/locations where you tend to pull.

You also learned how to make your *Weekly Chart* by reviewing your *Problem Solving Chart* and transferring the information to the *Weekly Chart* format. By checking it on a daily basis you will easily be able to keep track of your progress.

We hope that you understand by now that **will power alone cannot control trich;** you need to structure your space and your activities so that your body's needs can be met without pulling! You also need to be aware of how often you are actually using your strategies. If you want to decrease pulling, **you must use your strategies on a daily basis**, even if you do not you have the urge to pull. Your *Weekly Chart* will help you keep track of whether or not you are doing what you need to do in order to trick trich!

In the next chapter we will show you how to set up a reward system to help motivate you when you actually (finally!) put your plan into action. Meanwhile, you have earned the **fifth piece of the puzzle!**

CHAPTER 6

GETTING AND STAYING MOTIVATED

INTRODUCTION

In the last chapter you learned how to set up your environment, and how to write a *Weekly Chart*. However, before you put your plan into place, there is one more thing that we would like you to do.

We recognize that managing your hair pulling problem will take a lot of self-discipline and motivation. In this chapter you will learn how you and your parents can set up a reward system to help keep you motivated. We think that you will like our ideas!

USING REWARDS

We have found that when people are highly motivated they are able to accomplish many difficult things. Knowing that you will feel happier and less self-conscious may be enough to keep you motivated to do the hard work that is involved in managing trich. However, many kids make better progress when they are able to earn **rewards** for using their strategies in trigger situations. This is called **positive reinforcement**, and it is one of the most powerful tools for helping people change. It is a tool that you and your parents can use together to help you solve the Tricking Trich Puzzle.

However, using a reward system is not always necessary in order to make progress. Therefore, you have several options: First, you can follow the reward system with your parents' help as we describe in this chapter. Second, you can reward yourself by using your own allowance to buy yourself prizes, or by letting yourself do certain things (like watching certain TV shows) as rewards for earning points. Third, earning the points can in itself be rewarding. Some kids find that using their checklist every day and seeing their progress gives them a lot of satisfaction, and that they do not necessarily need to earn rewards. Whatever you decide, remember that you need to be **motivated** in order to manage trich, so find a way to get your motivation high and to keep it there!

MAKING A WISH LIST

We will begin by asking you some questions: how would you like the chance to earn some rewards such as money, games, clothes, and cosmetics? What about extra privileges such as special outings, inviting a friend to the movies, or staying up late? If you could have a *Wish List* of rewards, what would you include?

On the next few pages are examples of two wish lists. Please read them carefully. The first is a general one. The second list is one that Sally wrote. Notice that both lists include things that cost money as well as rewards that do not cost money. Also notice that in both cases there are groupings of "small," "medium," and "large" rewards. After you read the lists, we would like you to make your own list, one that includes things that are important or interesting to you. The idea is for you to come **up with rewards that you would like a chance to earn.**

****

IDEAS FOR A WISH LIST

SMALL REWARDS (able to earn at least one per day)

Objects:

gum	candy
hair ornaments	stickers
nail polish	choice of a small prize from a
small amounts of money	grab bag

Privileges:

special time with mom or dad	skip a chore
five minute back rub	manicure from mom
special bubble bath	borrow mom's perfume or
	cosmetics

MEDIUM REWARDS (can be earned in 4-7 days)

Objects:

paperback book	new socks or nylons
costume jewelry	art supplies
cosmetics	add an item to a collection

Privileges:

extra use of car (if you are a
   driver)
rent a video
friend over for overnight

out for ice cream with a friend
roller skating
in charge of TV for the evening
out to the movies

LARGE REWARDS   (can be earned in 2-4 weeks)

Objects:

an article of clothing
small pet
a CD

jewelry
collectible
money

Privileges:

"Queen or King for a Week"
   (no chores for one week)
party
haircut
make-over

special outing (e.g. amusement
   park)
mini-vacation (e.g. day trip to a
   nearby city)
dinner out at a fun place

****

As you can see, there are many things that you can put on a wish list. Some of them are things that you may already get for "free," but perhaps not too often. Other rewards might include things that you ordinarily would not be allowed to do or have. The reward system would give you an opportunity to earn more privileges, objects, special outings, or anything else that you and your parents can agree on.

Sally and her parents have agreed to work on a reward system to help her manage TTM. The first step is for Sally to write out her *Wish List*:

I really enjoyed reading about having a Wish List. It's fun to think about things I might be able to earn. My Wish List will

include some things that I already get to do on occasion but would like to do more often (like staying up past my regular bedtime or renting a video tape) as well as some things that I want to be able to buy. My parents do not have a lot of extra money, so I will mostly ask for privileges and inexpensive rewards. But I also will ask my parents if I can include a few expensive things that I would usually get on special occasions (like going out to dinner). I also really want to get my nose pierced, and I hope they will let me do that as a really big reward. I'll write up my list, talk to my parents, and let you know what we come up with.

Sally completed her *Wish List* and discussed it with her parents. On the next page is the list of rewards that they agreed upon.

SALLY'S WISH LIST

Small Rewards (can earn at least one every day):

Stickers
Candy
Stay up 30 minutes past bedtime
Skip a chore
Hair ornament
Choose a dessert

Medium Rewards (can be earned in 4-7 days):

Choose a dinner
Paperback book
New socks
Costume jewelry
Out for an inexpensive lunch

Large Rewards (can be earned in 2-4 weeks):

Get second holes in my ears
Out to dinner
Jewelry
Makeover

As you can see, I was able to think of quite a few rewards for myself. My parents agreed to everything except getting my nose pierced, so that got dropped from my list. However, as a compromise, they did agree that I could get a second pierced

hole in my ear (I already have one in each ear) as a large reward. It was fun talking and planning together, and having some things to look forward to.

Go ahead and write a Wish List and discuss it with your parents. It's fun!

☞☞☞ At this point you probably have a pretty good idea about how to write your own *Wish List*. Please turn to the *Wish List* form in the Appendix on page A-167. Write up your list and then continue with this chapter.

THE POINT SYSTEM

☞☞☞ Now that you have written a *Wish List* that you and your parents agree on, you are ready to go on to the next step. Get out your *Weekly Chart* from Chapter 5 (Page A-157), which you have already filled out. Sit down with your parents and go over your *Weekly Chart* with them. Count the number of strategies that you have listed in your *Weekly Chart* (we recommend that you list 6-12 strategies per day.)

Next, decide how many points you will get for using each strategy. Most kids arrange with their parents to earn a point (up to a certain maximum) every time they use a strategy. For example, if you wrote down that you will play with Silly Putty when you watch TV in the family room, then you should be able to earn a point **each time** that you play with Silly Putty for a few minutes. You may earn 2, 3, or more points per day for using that particular strategy in the family room, depending on your arrangement with your parents. In this way, with the 6-12 strategies that you will be working on daily, you will be able to earn about 15-20 points **each day.** Now take your *Weekly Chart* and write down the number of points that you can earn for using each strategy.

On the next page is Sally Sample's *Weekly Chart,* which now includes the number of points that Sally can earn by using her strategies.

SALLY'S WEEKLY CHART (INCLUDING POINTS): Date Started _____

LOCATION/ACTIVITY	STRATEGY	POINTS	S	M	T	W	T	F	S
Family Room									
• watching TV	Play with Silly Putty (F)	1-3							
	Wear rubber fingers (H)	1							
	Sit in a different chair (E)	1							
Bathroom	Wash face with textured sponge								
	(E)	1							
	Cover mirror (E)	1							
Bedroom									
• doing homework	Play with mushroom brush (S)	1-3							
	Brush hair (S)	1-3							
• getting ready for bed	Wear Band-Aids (H)	2							
• talking on phone	Make beaded earrings (F)	3							
	Wear ponytail (H)	2							
	Use my strategies (P)	1-3							

Points Earned Today:	
+ **Balance Forward:**	
Subtotal:	
- Points Spent:	
NEW BALANCE:	

F = Fiddle
S = Meet your **Sensory** needs
H = Make it **Hard** to pull
E = Change your **Environment**
E(m) =Deal with your **Emotions** in a better way
P = Don't be **Perfectionistic**

☞☞☞   Now turn to your *Wish List* (A-167). Guided by the number of points that you can earn each day, you and your parents can now decide on and write down the number of points that each reward will "cost." You should be able to earn at least one small reward in one day, a medium reward in 4-7 days and a large reward in 2-4 weeks. For super large rewards, you may need to work for several months. One family who was financially able to do so offered a trip to Disney World as an incentive. The boy had to work for six months in order to earn the reward, but he did it! For most families this would not be possible. More typically, a large reward might be something that can be earned in about 2-4 weeks, such as an article of clothing worth $10-$20.

At this point, Sally Sample and her parents decided on the number of points that Sally could earn for using her strategies. They also got out her *Wish List*, and worked out the number of points each item on her list would cost. They agreed that at the beginning, Sally should be able to earn at least one small reward each day. This would keep her motivated. If she were perfect, she could earn 15-20 points a day. But Sally would not have to be perfect in order to earn a reward!! The rewards would be a happy reminder when she was using her strategies well (good job!), and a gentle, not so happy reminder when she did not use her strategies.

On the next page is Sally's revised *Wish List*, which now <u>includes</u> the number of points that each reward will "cost":

SALLY'S WISH LIST (*INCLUDING POINTS*)

Small Rewards:

Stickers **(5 pts)**
Candy **(5 pts)**
Stay up 15-30 minutes past bedtime (**5-8 pts**)
Skip a chore **(6 pts)**
Hair ornament **(8 pts)**
Choose a dessert **(5 pts)**

Medium Rewards:

Choose a dinner **(20 pts)**
Paperback book **(25 pts)**
New socks **(20 pts)**
Costume jewelry **(30 pts)**
Quiet voice from family **(30 pts)**
Out for an inexpensive lunch **(35 pts)**
Have a sleepover party **(70 pts)**

Large Rewards:

Get a second pierced hole in my ear **(200 pts)**
Out to dinner **(200 pts)**
Jewelry **(100-200 pts)**
Makeover **(200 pts)**

Developing a point system is complicated. If you are still a little confused about how the reward system works, go back and review Sally's forms again. Notice, for instance, that on her *Weekly Chart* she has written down that she plans to use Silly Putty (1pt), wear rubber fingers (1pt), and sit in a different chair (1pt) when she is watching TV in the family room. That will give her three points. At the end of the day, Sally will add up all of her points. These points will be used to earn rewards on her *Wish List*.

You and your parents should try to come up with a system that you all feel comfortable with. Expect that you will need to modify it over time, especially if you are earning too many rewards. Remember that you should be challenged (but not <u>too</u> challenged), and that your parents should not be spending too much money!

KEEPING TRACK OF YOUR POINTS

Once your system is set up, you will need to keep track of what you have earned as well as what you have spent. You can do this by filling out the bottom area of your *Weekly Chart*. Add up the number of points that you earn each day, plus the number of points that you carried over from the day or week before. Then subtract the number of points that you spent on your rewards that day. The bottom line is your new "balance," which you can save for future rewards.

Sally will keep her *Weekly Chart* and *Wish List* **together in a visible place**. That way she can use them easily and keep track of her progress. Please do the same with yours.

WRITING A CONTRACT

Now that you have come up with your agreement, it is time to write a *Contract* with your parents. The *Contract* will be an agreement of good faith. It will show that you will make a commitment to work hard, and that your parents will support your efforts by letting you earn rewards. Here is the form that Sally and her parents wrote out:

<u>CONTRACT</u>

I, _____*Sally*_____ AGREE TO TRY TO USE THE STRATEGIES ON MY WEEKLY LIST. I WILL WRITE DOWN MY POINTS EVERY DAY IN ORDER TO KEEP TRACK OF HOW I AM DOING.

MY PARENTS AGREE TO LET ME TRADE IN MY POINTS FOR THE ITEMS ON MY WISH LIST.

_____*Sally*_____   _____*Jan. 3*_____
  My   Signature   Date

_____*Susan (Mom), Jack (Dad)*_____   _____*Jan. 3*_____
  Parent   Signature   Date

☞☞☞   We would like you to write a *Contract* with your parents, too. You can use the blank one on page A-169, or you can make up your own.

WHY GIVE REWARDS FOR USING STRATEGIES?

You may want to know why we recommend that you earn points for **using strategies** instead of for hair growth or for not **pulling.**

Well, the reason is a very important one: we want you to focus on the **positive things you can do instead of pulling your hair**. If you keep on using lots of strategies **based on your needs**, then you will be much less likely to pull your hair.

In addition, we know that even if you have an excellent week or month, "slips" can cause a lot of damage to your hair in a matter of minutes. This does **not** mean that you are back to square one! Remember that you are working on changing your behavior and that you're not going to be perfect. You **will** "slip" from time to time. But you should still get your points for using your strategies! If you get rewarded for behaviors that help you decrease pulling, eventually you will gain more control over your habit and manage your "slips" better. As a result, your hair will begin to grow back. Does that make sense to you? We hope so!

SUMMARY

In this chapter, we explained that if you are highly motivated you should be able to decrease, and maybe even eliminate, hair pulling. We showed you how to set up a reward system with your parents so that you can earn rewards for using your strategies. Setting up the system will take some work, but as we have shown you, it will also be fun! By completing this chapter, you have earned the **sixth piece of the Tricking Trich Puzzle!**

In the next chapter you will begin **carrying out your plan to trick trich**. You will also learn how to make changes in your plan over time. It has taken a while to get to this point, for tricking trich takes a lot of knowledge and preparation. But you know what? **You are ready, now!** So, let's begin!

CHAPTER 7

PUTTING YOUR PLAN
INTO ACTION

INTRODUCTION

☞ ☞ ☞ At this point, we hope that you have finished doing the tasks listed below. Please place a "checkmark" or star next to the things that you have already done. If there are any that you have **not** done so far, go back and do them before working on this chapter:

___Completed your *Information About My Pulling Chart* (Chapter 2);

___Read about and chosen some strategies that you might like to try (Chapter 3);

___Worked on your *Problem Solving Chart* (Chapter 4);

___Gathered your supplies and set up your environment (Chapter 5);

___Written your first *Weekly Chart* (Chapter 5); and

___Written a *Wish List* and your first *Contract* with your parents (Chapter 6).

If you have completed these tasks, you are now ready to put your

91

plan into action. You should be impressed with all the hard work that you have done, and all that you have learned! In this chapter you will learn how to put your plan into action and how to modify it over the next several weeks.

WEEK ONE: TRYING OUT YOUR PLAN

We would like you to try your plan for one week. Give the plan a chance, even if some things do not work as well as you would like them to. At the end of one week you will have some ideas about what works and what needs to be changed.   No matter how carefully a plan has been set up, it usually does need some changes!

A ten-year old who was in therapy worked very hard to recognize her trigger situations, and to come up with a plan to manage her pulling. With her therapist's help, she and her parents wrote a contract with a reasonable reward system to help her stay motivated. The reward system was set up so that the girl would earn about ten points each day as long as she worked hard at it, but without her having to be perfect. The following week the child came back to therapy to report on her progress. She very proudly announced that she had done much better than anyone had anticipated. In fact, she had earned about seventy points a day. "At this rate," she said, "at the end of the month I'll earn a new car!" Everyone agreed that the plan was good, but that the reward system needed to be more challenging.

The plan was adjusted so that the girl could only earn around ten points per day. This was done by increasing the number of times a strategy had to be used in order to earn a point. For instance, she now had to use certain strategies three times in order to earn a point instead of just once. After several more adjustments over a period of weeks, her plan was very effective. She earned a lot of nice things without breaking the bank!

Let's look at the next page to see how Sally's *Weekly Chart* looked at the end of her first week:

SALLY'S WEEKLY CHART (INCLUDING POINTS):   Date Started _____

LOCATION/ACTIVITY	STRATEGY	POINTS	S	M	T	W	T	F	S
Family Room									
• watching TV	Play with Silly Putty (F)	1-3	1	1		1			
	Wear rubber fingers (H)	1			1			1	1
	Sit in a different chair (E)	1					1		
Bathroom	Wash face with textured sponge (S)	1		1					
	Cover mirror (E)	1	1	1	1	1	1	1	1
Bedroom									
• doing homework	Play with mushroom brush (S)	1		1		1	1	1	
	Brush hair (S)	1-3	3	2	2	3	3	2	3
	Wear Band-Aids (H)	2	2	2		2		2	
• getting ready for bed	Make beaded earrings (F)	3							3
• talking on phone	Wear ponytail (H)	2	2	2		2	2		
	Use my strategies (P)	1-3	1	1	1	1	1	1	1

		S	M	T	W	T	F	S
Points Earned Today:		8	11	5	9	8	8	9
+ Balance Forward:		0	+3	+4	+4	+10	+15	+8
Subtotal:		8	14	9	13	18	23	17
- Points Spent:		-5	-10	-5	-3	-3	-15	-10
NEW BALANCE:		3	4	4	10	15	8	7

F = Fiddle
S = Meet your **Sensory** needs
H = Make it **Hard** to pull
E = **Change your Environment**
E(m) = Deal with your **Emotions** in a better way
P = Don't be **Perfectionistic**

WEEKS TWO AND THREE: REVIEWING AND REVISING

Now that you have tried out your plan for one week, ask yourself these questions: Did I have to work too **hard** to earn the points? Was it too **easy** to earn points? Did I receive a small reward every day? Did I increase my self-awareness? Did I actually change my hair pulling behavior?

Remember that by using your *Weekly Chart and Wish List* you should be challenged and rewarded on a **day to day** basis. If the system is working correctly, you should be able, with effort, to earn one or two **small** rewards each day. If you are not able to earn a small reward every day, then the reward system is too hard for you, and should be adjusted. If you are earning too many rewards, then your contract should be changed so that it will be harder to earn rewards.

Hopefully, your awareness regarding your pulling behavior increased the first week. Maybe you stopped yourself from pulling by **being more aware** that you were touching your hair, and quickly grabbed and played with a Koosh Ball for a few minutes. Or maybe you **remembered** to put a hat on before you started watching TV. If you were successful in these ways, that is great! But even if you pulled your hair, and **then** remembered that you were supposed to be wearing Band-Aids in that room, your increased awareness still helped you because you could ask yourself the question, **"What can I do differently next time?"** This kind of problem solving and planning is the most important way for you to trick trich!

When you review your *Weekly Chart* at the end of the first week you may decide that it needs to be changed in some way. For instance, let's say that during the first week you realize that you sometimes pull your hair in the bathroom after brushing your teeth. At this point you may want to add some strategies (like flossing your teeth or covering the mirror) to your *Weekly Chart.* These kinds of changes are to be expected. After all, tricking trich is a learning process! Over the next few weeks you will continue to modify your *Weekly Chart* until you find a combination of strategies that work or you.

By about the third week, you should be a "pro" at earning small rewards. Now is a good time to start working towards some **medium sized rewards** that can be earned on a weekly, rather than a daily, basis. Making this change means that you will need to wait several days for your reward even though you will be working on using your strategies on a day to day basis. If this is very difficult for you to do, you might want to use some of your points for daily rewards while saving the rest for medium rewards. Another way that you can get daily "reinforcement" while saving your points for larger rewards is to earn "part" of the larger reward each day.

One boy we know wanted to get a certain board game as his reward. This was a medium sized reward, which would take 7-10 days to earn. However, he needed to have some reinforcement on a daily basis to help him stay motivated. He and his parents solved the problem by drawing a picture of the game on a piece of construction paper, and then cutting the piece of paper into ten pieces. Each day he was able to earn enough points for one or two pieces. After nine days he had earned all the pieces, taped them together to make the complete picture, and got to go to the store and buy the game!

WEEKS FOUR AND FIVE: GETTING IN THE GROOVE

By the end of the first month or so, you might notice that some of the strategies that you have been using have made it easy for you to resist pulling in certain trigger settings. Maybe your urge has decreased in those situations so much that you are not too tempted to pull in those situations. That is very good news!

However, other trigger situations may have proven more challenging, and in still others you may not have been successful at all. Guess what? **It is time to change your** *Weekly Chart* **again!** Remove the strategies from your chart that have become easy for you. **That does not mean that you will stop using the strategies in those trigger situations!!** You must **continue to use them,** at least for several more weeks, to be sure that your pulling behavior in those trigger situations is under control. However, you do not need to be earning points for using them. Instead, **add more or different strategies, or give yourself more points for using strategies in the tougher situations.**

Hi! In the first few weeks, although I had to change my chart a few times, I started to notice that I was pulling a lot less. This made me feel great. But after two or three weeks, I noticed that the chart was not working as well as it had at

first. At that point I decided that I was not really interested any more in earning daily rewards. I also noticed that I had better control over pulling in some trigger situations than in others. For instance, I no longer pulled when I was talking on the phone, but that was still on my Weekly Chart.   I was doing a lot better with the pulling in the family room, but I was still having trouble in my bedroom.

The next thing I needed to do was to redo my chart. Since I now automatically used my strategies when I was talking on the phone, I removed those strategies from my chart. At the same time, I decided to choose some new strategies when sitting in the family room, because I noticed that I was getting bored with the old ones. But I only gave myself one point for using each strategy in that room because it was a pretty "easy" trigger situation for me to manage.

The bedroom, on the other hand, was still really hard for me. I decided to choose some new strategies and to give myself <u>two</u> points every time that I used one of them when I was in that room. This helped to perk me up and gave me a better chance to earn my rewards!

I also decided to choose some bigger and more interesting rewards that would take me longer to earn. My medium sized choices were to invite a friend out for ice cream (I could earn that in about three days), to get a manicure (I could earn that in around five days), and to go out to one of my favorite restaurants for lunch (I could earn that in seven or eight days).

After making these changes, I made even more rapid progress. The changes made such a big difference! I know now that every few weeks I will need to look at my plan and decide whether any changes need to be made. If I have a hard day or week I know that I will probably need to change my Weekly Chart again so that I can get back on track quickly.

WEEKS SIX AND SEVEN: KEEPING UP THE GOOD WORK

At this point, look at your *Weekly Chart* **again**. Are there any more strategies or positive behaviors on your chart that have become easy for you to do? If there are, **remove them from the *Weekly Chart* and replace them with more difficult challenges.** (But be sure to save your old *Weekly Charts* so you can look back at how far you have come!) Think about additional medium-sized rewards, as well as large rewards that you can work toward over the next few weeks. See if you are getting bored with any of the strategies. If so, look at the *Strategies List* in Chapter 3 and **try some different strategies in the rooms where you are still pulling.** Buy some new supplies. Move alternatives from one room to another. Be creative!

One high school girl found that polishing her nails was an excellent strategy for her. At first, she just kept nail polish in her bedroom. Once she realized how well it worked for her, she put nail polish, cotton balls, and small bottles of nail polish remover in all of her strategy baskets around the house, as well as next to each telephone. She also put a hand towel in each basket to put the nail polish bottle on so she would not have to worry about spills. She enjoyed buying new colors when she went out with her mother to buy new things for her strategy baskets. She kept hand lotion and cotton gloves in her room to use each night, and guess what? She started getting lots of compliments on how beautiful her hands looked! But she remembered that it was really important to use other strategies as well, so she also continued to keep and use different supplies such as Koosh Balls, scarves, and Band-Aids.

WEEKS EIGHT-SIXTEEN: STAYING ON TRACK

For the next three months or so you will be changing your *Weekly Chart* a couple of times a month until you find combinations **of strategies and rewards that work for you.** You should also update your *Problem Solving Chart* every so often as well, so that you stay aware of your different needs and the different kinds of strategies that meet those needs.

Remember to **keep on using the strategies that work for you, even if they are no longer on your chart**, at least until you are sure that you can be in control without them in those settings. To be on the safe side, continue to use them on a regular basis for at least a month. And keep those hand and mouth or sensory strategies nearby, even when you do not need to use them on a regular basis. Remember that **pulling has served a purpose**, and even if you have controlled your pulling behavior, your body still has its needs! The idea is to meet those needs in constructive ways. So if you are a **fiddler**, keep on playing with that silly putty when you watch TV. If your scalp needs **sensory attention**, brush your hair when you are on the telephone, even when you are not tempted to pull!

One seven-year-old boy pulled in his hair when he was at church and in Sunday School class. He was an active kid who loved playing and watching sports, especially hockey. Having to sit quietly in a chair for a few hours at a time was boring for him. He decided to use three basic strategies: First, he wore a baseball hat during Sunday School class. Second, in order to get rid of his extra energy, he ran laps around the church before services. And third, (after agreeing not to throw them in the air) he took some of his "toys" into church so he could play with them during church services if he needed to. He earned many points for using these strategies, which he traded in for a lot of nice rewards (including getting to go to a professional hockey game!) He made excellent progress and was eventually able to be less dependent on needing to wear his baseball hat.

Even after gaining control over his pulling, he **still** had a need to have things to fiddle with, and he still had to tire himself out before church so that he did not feel so fidgety during services. Therefore, his parents continued to give him points for using those strategies. They also gave him points for getting good reports from the Sunday School teacher. In this way, his reward system was adapted to meet his body's needs in quiet settings, even when pulling was no longer a problem for him.

After working on your plan for several weeks you are now more self-aware, self-disciplined, and creative in tricking trick. You will probably slip from time to time, but that is to be expected. Just remember to always ask yourself, **"What can I do differently next time?"** Whatever your answer is to that question, **do it!** If you get stuck, go back and review the earlier chapters.

PHASING OUT USE OF THE WEEKLY CHART

If managing your hair pulling has become routine at this point, you may no longer need the structure of using the *Weekly Chart*. If you choose to do so, you can phase the chart out. However, this should be a process that is gradually and carefully done, and you should be prepared to return to using the chart whenever needed. Remember that the weekly chart is your guide and your friend!

MODIFYING THE POINT/REWARD SYSTEM

The basic way that the point/reward system is set up is for you to start out earning small rewards, and then to "graduate" to medium and large rewards. However, some families like to work their system differently. Some parents, for instance, give their kids their small rewards, but do not subtract the points from the balance. Instead, the points continue to be accumulated towards medium sized rewards. In this way, the child is not "charged" for the small rewards. Another way of doing this would be to say that when a kid earns ten small rewards she could get a medium reward. Younger kids often like this system because then they don't have to wait so long in order to get rewarded for their hard work.

Many teens are able to skip the small rewards altogether, and to start out with working towards medium rewards. The most important thing is to find a system that you and your parents like and that works for you!

SUMMARY

In this chapter you learned how to put your plan into action, and in doing so you have earned the **seventh piece of the Tricking Trich Puzzle**! You learned that it is important to **follow your plan** while also being **flexible** and **creative**. You have the *Problem Solving Chart, Weekly Chart,* and your **reward system** to guide and motivate you. Use them for as long as they are helpful. Here is what the puzzle looks like now!

In Chapter 8 you will learn about managing trich over the long run. We will also show you how to get back on track when slips occur. Look at how far you've come!

CHAPTER 8

HOLDING YOUR OWN

INTRODUCTION

In the last chapter you learned how put your plan into action. You found out that by making needed changes over time you learned a lot about what works and what does not work for you. In this chapter we will look at the progress that you may already have made, and will discuss ways for you to hold on to your gains.

LONG TERM GOALS

Now that you have used your plan for a number of weeks, you may have noticed a decrease in your pulling behavior. However, it is also possible that you have not yet noticed any changes in your hair pulling behavior. Whatever your degree of success so far, your goal should be to **manage** (not cure) trich by finding better ways to meet your body's needs. **You will probably always have those needs, and the better you are at meeting them, the better you will be at managing your hair pulling problem.**

GETTING BACK ON TRACK WHEN YOU SLIP

Once hair pulling has decreased, some people think that they will never have to think about their hair pulling again. This attitude creates a false sense of security and is a big mistake! The fact is, **it is likely that you may always have a tendency to pull your hair.** It is very possible that the urge to pull could sneak up on you "out of the blue," and if you are not prepared, you could resume pulling. Even if you are prepared, "slips" can happen at any time.

When you do slip, go back to your *Information About My Pulling Checklist* and ask yourself these questions: "Where was I when I pulled? What happened before I pulled my hair? What did I do after I pulled the first few hairs? Are the triggers new or are they already on my list?"

If your hair pulling pattern is basically the **same** as it was before, then review your plan. If you have stopped using it, you may need to go back to using your plan, at least until you are back in control of your pulling for several weeks. You might use the same exact plan that you used before, or you might decide to change it in some way.

If your hair pulling pattern has **changed**, then you may need to expand or change your plan. You may need to redo your chart, come up with new strategies, and/or change your contract with your parents.

Continued self-awareness, self-discipline, and problem solving are the keys to your success. Remember, the most important ways that you will maintain your gains are: 1) to accept that it is very likely that you will continue to pull from time to time, and 2) to know what to do to get back on track when you slip.

We know a teenager who, after having successfully developed a plan, had not pulled her hair for one whole year. Then, she started to pull a little bit. After a few weeks, she noticed that she was pulling her hair a bit more each day. Before the pulling got too bad, she looked back at the plan that she had used the previous year. She returned to using some of the strategies that had worked for her in the past. After two weeks of using her old strategies, she got her hair pulling back under control, and was able to put her charts away again until next time!

WHEN YOUR OLD STRATEGIES AREN'T ENOUGH

If you need to return to using your *Problem Solving Chart* and *Weekly Chart*, you might find that some of the strategies that used to work so well do not work any more. There are many reasons why this could happen. Sometimes, it is just a matter of **boredom.** Using the same strategies over and over may work well for some people, but you may need more variety or a different angle on things. Sometimes, strategies that worked really well one year may not work that well again the following year because **you are older and need something different**. And sometimes we just don't know why strategies that used to work don't work anymore.

If your old strategies are not working, do **not** give up! There are many, many strategies and combinations of strategies out there that you have not tried yet. **If you keep trying, you should be able to**

make progress!   And if you have already had some success, then you **know** that if you could do it once, you can do it again!

A nine-year old girl worked very hard at identifying her triggers, making a *Problem Solving Chart*, developing a plan, and writing a contract with her parents. After a long struggle, she made excellent progress in controlling her pulling. Gradually, she was able to decrease her dependence on her checklists, charts, and contracts. She felt so much better about herself and was very proud of her accomplishment!

However, about eight months later, she found herself starting to pull again. Right away, she got out her book and reviewed it. She noticed that most of the trigger situations were the same, but there were one or two that were different. She started using her old strategies that had worked so well for her before. Some of them continued to be effective, but most of the others were not helping her as much as they had done previously. She looked at the *Comprehensive Strategies List* in her book, and found several ideas that she had not used in the past. She then revised her *Problem Solving* and *Weekly* charts to include these new strategies. She went back to using her *Weekly Chart* and Point System, so that she could get back on track. A month later, she was back in control. She had done a good job of tricking trich!

EXPECTATIONS OVER THE LONG RUN

Over the long run, you will need to be flexible and open-minded when it comes to managing trichotillomania. Going back to using your charts does **not** mean that you have failed. It will just be a reminder that you need some extra problem solving ideas and more structure. **Expect** that you will need to go back to using them from time to time, and try to think about your continued efforts as opportunities to be creative and maybe even to have some fun!

As you probably remember from the previous chapters, I used a lot of great ideas from my Problem Solving Chart so that I could design and use a really good Weekly Chart. Things began to work pretty well. The most helpful strategies for me were using the rubber fingers when I was watching TV, wearing Band-Aids at night, wearing my hair in a pony tail, and washing my face with a textured sponge. I enjoyed being more in control of my pulling, and I also enjoyed earning make-up, some clothes, and a special weekend with a friend. It was a lot of work, but it was worth it, because over the next several months I slowly reduced my hair pulling until it was no longer a major problem.

Everything went fine for a while. Then I got tired of using all of the strategies, and soon I began not bothering to use them at all. I thought that I'd be OK because I still wasn't pulling too much. During the next few months, though, I noticed that I was pulling my hair more and more, hoping that I could get back in control without having to go back to using my charts.

Finally, I did so much damage that I had to cover up my hair with a scarf to hide my bald spots. I felt so frustrated! But before I let myself get too discouraged, I thought to myself, "I tricked trich once and I can do it again. All I have to do is to start doing something to get back on track! After all, doing anything is better than doing nothing."

Once I gave myself that pep talk, I filled out a Trich Review Form (see page 112) and got out my old charts. I was surprised to see how many helpful strategies I used to use that I had just let slip away. I reviewed and modified my Problem Solving Chart, and then wrote up a new Weekly Chart. I began to use my old strategies again, including wearing Band-Aids at night and playing with Silly Putty or wearing rubber fingers while I watched TV. I also resumed wearing my hair in a ponytail and washing my face with a textured sponge.

These things helped, but I wanted some new ideas, too. I looked up the Comprehensive Strategies List in Chapter 3 and added some new strategies to my plan: getting a massage brush and brushing my hair with it at least eight times a day, and polishing my nails a few times every week. I found that using both the old and the new strategies really helped me.

In less than two weeks I was back in control of my pulling. At that point I was able to gradually decrease use of the chart. After a few more weeks, I was able to get down to only two strategies, which I am still using: wearing rubber fingers and keeping my hands busy while watching TV. Even though I feel like I am in good control and the urge is getting weaker, I will continue using those two strategies for the next couple of months, just to be on the safe side. And I will keep a basket of toys in the family room, just in case.

At this point my hair has grown back enough so that I no longer need to wear a scarf. It will take a few months for my hair to be full again, but I did it before, so I can do it again. I just need to be patient and to stay alert.

I have learned the hard way that trich can be tricky! I am proud of myself for getting back on track, but boy, next time I'll know to catch myself sooner! I hope that you will remember to do the same.

Sally has learned that slips will occur. But instead of getting discouraged or overwhelmed, she filled out a *Trich Review Form* so that she could help herself. Look at the next page to see what she wrote, then fill in the form (see page A-171) if and when you need to:

TRICH REVIEW FORM

Date ***June 1***

Here are the trigger situations (location, time of day, and activities) where I am having problems. ***Watching TV in family room, bedtime.***

By answering these questions I can help myself get back on track:

1) Is my *Problem Solving Chart* up to date (does it include my current triggers)? ***Yes.*** If not, what needs to be changed? _____

_____

2) Do I need to use my *Weekly Chart* more regularly? ***Yes.*** Does it include my current trigger situations? ***Yes.*** Am I keeping track of my points? ***No.***

3) Does my *Weekly Chart* have enough different kinds of strategies? ***Not sure.*** Note what they are and if I am using them every day:

Fiddling ***Silly Putty***		***No***
Sensory ***Wash face with textured sponge***		***No***
Hard to pull ***Rubber fingers, Band-Aids at night, pony tail***		***No***
Environment ***Sit in a different chair in family room***		***Yes***
Emotion ***Not a problem at this time***		
Perfectionism ***Not a problem at this time***		

4) Does my reward system need to be "beefed up"? ***No.*** If so, how?

_____

5) What new strategies or supplies do I need to add? ***Get and use massage brush several times a day (S), polish fingernails a few times per week (F).***

6) The next time I have the urge to pull, what should I do differently so I can prevent an episode or at least minimize the damage that I do? ***Grab my alternatives, look at my chart, get up and go where other people are.***

GETTING EXTRA HELP

Now that you have been through all the steps of the program, we hope that you have a feeling of greater control over your hair pulling. But as you can see, trich **can** sneak back up on you, even if you have not pulled for months. Trying your "old" strategies may work for you. If not, try adding some new ones. If you have never worked with a therapist and would like some extra help, then you and your parents may want to get in touch with a counselor, social worker, psychologist, or psychiatrist. If you have gotten professional help in the past, you may want to go back to your therapist and get some "booster" sessions. You may only need a few!

A high school boy who was in therapy for about six months learned how to successfully manage his hair pulling. About one year after leaving therapy he started to pull his hair again. He tried to use some of the "old" techniques that had worked for him in the past. This time, those strategies did not really help very much. He then tried adding some new strategies, but still was not able to bring his pulling under control. Before things got too bad, he decided to go back to his old therapist for help. With his therapist's guidance, he did some good problem solving, and recognized some new triggers that he had not noticed. Soon, he had enough new ideas and strategies to maintain his gains on his own.

SUMMARY

In this chapter you have learned how important it is for you to notice if and when hair pulling is starting to be a problem for you again. If it is, you can then go back to using your charts for a while, and maybe revise them to meet your changing needs. **Making needed adjustments in your plan and using a variety of strategies** is a great sign of good management.

You may never pull again, but if you do (and most people do), you can figure out how to handle the problem and get back on track, either on your own or with the help of a therapist. You now have the **eighth piece of the Tricking Trich Puzzle**. Only one more piece and your puzzle will be complete.

In the next chapter we will review some of the highlights of this program, and you will see how much you have learned!

CHAPTER 9

LOOKING BACK AND PLANNING AHEAD

INTRODUCTION

In Chapter 8 we reminded you about how important it is to think about **managing** trich, not curing it. This is because pulling your hair has become an automatic behavior that has met certain needs. As you have met your needs in other ways and have learned how to use strategies that work for you, **it has become less and less necessary for you to pull your hair.** We also explained that even after you have gained better control over hair pulling, you will need to be alert so that trich does not "sneak up" on you. Finally, we discussed how to get yourself back on track when you have slipped.

In this chapter you will earn the **ninth** and **final** piece of the Tricking Trich Puzzle. This will be an easy chapter because basically we will just highlight the work that you have already done.

WHAT HAVE YOU LEARNED?

By this time you have learned that even though it is not easy, there are some very good ways to trick trich. Let's review some of the most important things for you to keep in mind:

- **Learning all you can about your unique hair pulling problem is necessary in order to manage trich.** The *Information About My Pulling Checklist* has already helped you learn about your hair pulling problem. You can continue to use it whenever you need to think more carefully when, where, and why you pull.

- **Using a good variety of strategies in each of your trigger situations, before you even get the urge to pull your hair, is also extremely important.** The *Strategies List* should continue to help you choose new and interesting strategies for almost any situation where you might be likely to pull your hair. If you are not sure about what kinds of strategies you need, think about "Fiddling Sheep"!

- **Planning ahead is essential.** Using the *Problem Solving Chart* and setting up baskets of supplies for your strategies where they are needed will prepare you for each trigger situation. Remember to use your strategies whether or not you have the urge to pull.

- **Using your *Weekly Chart* is the key to learning how to manage hair pulling.** It will help you keep track of your progress as well as your points!

- **Receiving rewards for using your strategies can be a fun way to help you stay on track.** Working out a **reward system with** your parents may help you stay motivated and focused.

- **Being a good problem solver will help you succeed with this program.** Rather than trying to never have setbacks, it's more important to accept that **you will slip from time to time.** Remember that you can use these experiences as learning opportunities. Ask yourself, **"What can I do differently next time?"** and take your own good advice! You may need to go back and re-read sections of this book, or re-do some of your charts and checklists. It's all part of tricking trich!

Reading about these important points reminds me that managing trich is a slow and complicated process, but by patiently following the step by step instructions in this book, I have learned how to be a good problem solver. This has helped me to meet my needs without pulling, and I now am managing trich with only minor and occasional slips. I will always need to stay alert, but I now know how to trick trich! I hope you do, too!

SUMMARY

In this chapter we have reviewed the key points involved in tricking trich! We think that you should be proud of all you have learned! You now have **all the pieces of the Tricking Trich Puzzle**! Here is the completed puzzle. Congratulations!

The next chapter is the last chapter in this book. In it we will give you a few last words of encouragement before we send you on your way!

CHAPTER 10

CONCLUSION: A FEW FINAL WORDS

At this point, we hope that your hair pulling is under pretty good control! But if it is not, then you have a choice: You can go through the program again--sometimes things "click" better the second time around. Or perhaps you are not quite ready to tackle this very tricky problem. If that is the case, it is perfectly fine if you choose to take a break from the program and try it again at a later time!

Whatever your rate of progress in managing trich, always remember that your trichotillomania is only a small part of who you are. If you are like most people with trich, you are a bright, creative, and caring person who has a variety of interests and hobbies. If you can accept and care for yourself as the worthwhile person we know you are, you **will be successful**, not only in in-increasing your ability to manage trich, but in every area of your life. We will let Sally have the last word, but we want you to know in closing, that we wish you the very best of luck in everything you do, now and always.

I can't believe that this is my last note to you. We sure have been through a lot together, haven't we? Getting through this book was both harder and more fun than I thought it would be. During the past few months I have learned a lot about myself and also about my habit. I also learned that if I have a good plan and use it

consistently, and if I keep on problem solving I can manage my hair pulling very well. At this point I generally do not have the urge to pull, but if and when I do, I will know what to do. If I do have setbacks, I will know how to get right back on track. I will have to continue being alert, but I am confident that trich will never be a big problem for me again, for I will always have this book to refer to if I need help.

The best thing about working on this program is that now that I am in better control of my pulling I can get on with my life! I am less self-conscious so I can enjoy school, friends, and sports more. I am also able to pay more attention to my cooking and horseback riding, now that I am not so focused on pulling. Finally, I am feeling more confident about myself. I now truly believe that I am worth taking good care of. You are worth it, too. Good luck and best wishes!

p.s. Drop me a line and let me know what you thought about the program and how you are doing!

My address is Sally Sample, c/o The Writers' Cooperative of Greater Washington, P.O. Box 10550, Silver Spring, MD 20914-0550.

PARENT GUIDE

PARENT GUIDE
TABLE OF CONTENTS

PARENT GUIDE

INTRODUCTION

If you are an adult reading this book, then you are probably the parent (or therapist) of a child who suffers from a disorder called **"trichotillomania."** Trichotillomania is a Latin-based word which describes non-cosmetic hair pulling. This book presents a comprehensive program that can help your child manage trichotillomania (which we also refer to as "trich" or "TTM"). The Parent Guide, which should be read in conjunction with the main part of the book, will:

1) give you general information about trichotillomania;

2) describe our approach to successfully managing TTM;

3) explain how you can be most helpful to your child as she proceeds through the book;

4) address the questions most commonly asked by parents of children with trichotillomania.

YOU AND YOUR CHILD

As we are sure you will agree, raising a child can be one of life's most rewarding experiences. It can also be extremely challenging at times. This is especially true when one's child is behaving in a perplexing manner that is not well understood by professionals, let alone by friends and members of the family. Having a child who pulls her hair is one of those situations, and can create a great sense of hopelessness and loneliness for both parent and child.

Many people, even some who suffer from TTM, may think that trichotillomania is a simple "bad habit" that can be controlled through will power or parental pressure alone. In actuality, the hair pulling problem is a complex one (which in many cases may be influenced by neurological factors) whose management requires a great deal of information, skill, organization, determination, and support.

You are reading this book because, in spite of her efforts, your child is simply not able to control her hair pulling at this time. Due to a lack of knowledge and skills, it is unlikely that she can anticipate or identify situations that trigger pulling, nor does she know about strategies that she can in order to prevent or end a pulling episode. In other words, she has neither the knowledge nor skills to control this powerful and emotionally painful problem.

Therefore, expectations that a child can "just stop," or that nagging or "catching her in the act" will solve the problem, are unrealistic. On the contrary, these attitudes can create power struggles, frustration, and feelings of helplessness in both parent and child.

However, the situation is **not** hopeless! Managing trichotillomania is a learning process that requires guidance, determina- tion and patience for both parents and children. But we have found that given the proper support, many parents **can help their children meet the challenge.**

ABOUT TRICHOTILLOMANIA

Since we strongly believe that knowledge is power, we want you to be knowledgeable regarding trichotillomania. Here is some background information that you should know:

- Researchers estimate that approximately 3% of the population suffers from trichotillomania. Most of those who seek treatment are girls or women; however, there is evidence that a significant percentage of people who pull their hair are males.

- On rare occasions, hair pulling can begin as early as infancy, when touching, stroking, twirling, and tugging on hair may occur as part of the normal tactile exploration of the environment. In some cases hair is actually pulled out. Most babies and young children outgrow this behavior, but for some, hair pulling becomes a behavior that can persist for many years.

- Most people with trichotillomania have their first pulling episode when they are between 9 and 14 years of age -- around the time of the onset of puberty. In some cases, however, the onset of TTM does not occur until late adolescence or adulthood.

- Once established, trichotillomania can quickly become extremely powerful. The problem may include specific patterns of behavior, such as playing with or biting the hairs or follicles. The severity of symptoms may wax and wane, and may be seasonal in nature.

- While preliminary research has shown a possible neurological basis for at least some people who suffer from trich, more knowledge is needed in order to fully understand trichotillo-mania. Meanwhile, there is no "cure" for trich, nor is there any one "magic bullet" approach that will work consistently. But the good news is that even without a complete medical understanding of trich, **the use of cognitive-behavioral strategies (such as the ones found in this book) and good problem solving skills** have been shown to help many people decrease and even eliminate hair pulling behavior.

HOW THIS BOOK CAN HELP YOUR CHILD

The program presented in this book will teach your child how to better manage her hair pulling problem.

- First, she will learn how to increase her awareness of her particular pulling patterns.

- Second, she will discover the many different idiosyncrasies of trichotillomania, and will identify which apply to her.

- Finally, she will learn how to develop a plan that she can use in various trigger situations to manage her urge to pull.

While TTM can be a chronic condition for some, **many young people with trichotillomania can learn to use the strategies in this book to help them manage their hair pulling behavior. Use of these strategies make it possible for them to reduce, and in**

some cases even eliminate, hair pulling, even into adulthood. With your help, your child may well have the same success!

HOW THIS BOOK CAN HELP YOU

With the help of this book, you will have an opportunity to be a valuable ally to your child, but perhaps in a different way than previously. If you have developed a way of interacting with your child around hair pulling behavior that you feel is not working, this book can help you change your involvement so that it is more constructive and helpful. This may be a difficult task for you, but remember that if your child can change patterns of behavior, so can you!

By reading and following the program in this book and parent guide, you will be able to help your child control her hair pulling problem. Specifically, you will:

1) Increase your knowledge about trichotillomania and how the disorder affects your child;

2) Learn how to help your child manage trich without nagging or scolding; and

3) Be able to design and develop an effective behavioral program that will motivate your child to decrease hair pulling behavior.

USING THIS BOOK

We recommend that both you and your child to **read the entire book before proceeding with the program.** Depending upon the age and ability of your child, you may find it necessary to read each chapter to or with her. There is a **great deal** of information in each chapter, and it may take up to a few weeks or even longer for your child to digest the information presented in the entire book. It is important for your child to be comfortable with the material and the approach before she begins. It may take her longer than it takes you. Please try to be patient.

In order to make this book as interesting and clear as possible, the book contains several "playful" devices. First, we used the concept of **solving a puzzle** as a metaphor for the problem solving process that we use. The message that we want your child to get is that there are many interlocking steps to managing trichotillomania, and that they are **all** important. We also want her to keep the "big picture" of problem solving in mind while she is working on each small step, which is similar to how one works on a jigsaw puzzle.

Another device is our use of the phrase **"tricking trich."** We use this phrase repeatedly throughout the book in order to illustrate that your child must develop a "bag of tricks" in order to effectively manage TTM. And like magicians, who have to keep up their practicing in order to "trick" their audiences, your child will need to develop certain skills and to **practice** using them on an ongoing basis.

In addition, we have included a mnemonic device: **"fiddling sheep."** This phrase should remind your child in a fun way that there are six main reasons why people pull their hair and six corresponding kinds of strategies: fiddling, sensory needs, hands have a mind of their own, emotions, environment, and perfectionism. It is important for several of these areas be addressed simultaneously to maximize the possibility of success. This device helps children make sure that they are using a wide range of strategies.

The last device that we use in the book is the creation of a fictional character named **"Sally Sample."** Sally has trich, and will go through the program, chapter by chapter, along with your child. She will go through some of the same struggles and victories that your child may also experience. We hope that Sally Sample's examples will clarify the concepts and tasks, and will inspire your child to do her best.

In the next section of the Parent Guide we will briefly discuss each chapter in the book, with an emphasis on how you can be a resource to your child at each step along the way. The comments do **not substitute for reading the chapters!**

COMMENTS REGARDING EACH CHAPTER

- ### CHAPTER 1: INTRODUCTION

This chapter is a basic introduction to trichotillomania. It contains information similar to that found in the Parent Guide, but written for a younger reader. You may simply want to be available to answer any questions (e.g., vocabulary or concepts) that your child may have. Your child will be asked to view trichotillomania in a new way, so it may take a little while for the information to "sink in." Be patient, and let your child take the time that she needs.

If your child wants to "rest" and not continue reading for a day or two (or even a week or two), let her. **Readiness** is a very important feature of this approach. Your child may not be quite ready to start this program, or there may be so much information in this (or any other) chapter that it may take a while to resonate with her. Pushing her to go ahead with the program when she is not ready may backfire and interfere with her success. If your child is resistant, the best thing to do is to make the book available and to encourage her to use it, but to respect your child's need to have some control regarding when to begin and how quickly to proceed.

• CHAPTER 2: GATHERING INFORMATION

This chapter was designed to raise your child's awareness regarding her particular pulling pattern, and includes an information gathering form, which she may want to keep private. Please try to respect your child's need for privacy. However, depending on your child's reading ability, she may require some help with the material. Try to be as helpful as you can be without asking your child to share more information than she is ready to give.

Your child's new level of awareness will evolve over time. You may find that she returns to this chapter several times during the course of this program.

• CHAPTER 3: LEARNING ABOUT STRATEGIES

This chapter has a great deal of key information. In fact, it contains the foundation of our treatment approach, and most of the chapters that follow will refer back to the information presented here. If any information in the remaining chapters is unclear, it will probably be helpful to review this chapter.

Because this chapter has so much information, your child might find it necessary to read it with you initially. Furthermore, she may find that it takes several days to plow through it. There is a lot to digest here, and it may take a few days for the information to "settle."

This chapter contains the "fiddling sheep" mnemonic device. Your child may enjoy using this device to memorize different kinds of strategies that she can use. Having this information at her fingertips will make it easier to come up with an effective plan later in the program.

- **CHAPTER 4: CREATING YOUR *PROBLEM SOLVING CHART***

This chapter uses the information gathered in Chapters 2 and 3 to complete a *Problem Solving Chart*. The chapter is self-explanatory. Again, you may need to help with reading or vocabulary.

- **CHAPTER 5: DEVELOPING YOUR PLAN**

In this chapter we will ask your child to use the information from Chapters 3 and 4 to create an overall management plan. She will be looking critically at various rooms in your house (as well as areas outside of the house), and setting up each "trigger" environment so that a variety of strategies are available to use as alternatives to pulling. The strategies may include tactile items, food items, writing materials, etc.

You will be asked to assist your child in gathering supplies that are already in the home, and purchasing some additional needed items. Most of the alternatives that we recommend are inexpensive; however, since we want your child to have supplies in several locations, the cost may add up. We hope that these purchases will be manageable for you. Do not hesitate to veto item requests that are beyond your budget or that you do not think are reasonable.

If your family has small children or energetic pets, you may need to establish rules regarding where the strategy supplies are kept. This will help insure that the child with trichotillomania is the one who actually uses them. Establishing a special shelf for your child that is out of the reach of toddlers, for example, may be helpful. Keeping some other toys handy for the other children in the family may be necessary to avoid hurt feelings. Every family has its own unique needs; finding a system that works for yours will be important in helping your child have unfettered access to her strategies.

Chapter 5 also describes how to write up a *Weekly Chart* so that progress can easily be tracked.

• CHAPTER 6: GETTING AND STAYING MOTIVATED

This chapter describes an aspect of the program where you will play an extremely important role: the development of a structured reward system. We truly believe that human behavior is largely shaped by using positive and negative consequences. In our "tricking trich" approach, we use **positive** rather than negative consequences. We do this because we have found that negative consequences (such as yelling, nagging, or punishing) simply do not help children to stop pulling their hair. **Positive reinforcement, on the other hand, has proven to be a very powerful tool in the battle against trichotillomania.**

By now you are fully aware that changing a complex behavior like trichotillomania requires a lot of hard work and perseverance. By using rewards, it will be easier to keep your child motivated through the long and difficult process of managing trich. At the same time, however, we understand that this aspect of the program may not be workable for every family. If that is true in your case, you may skip this chapter and proceed to the next.

Assuming that you do decide to use a reward system (and we hope that you will), it is very important to follow the plan outlined in this chapter. First, your child should "brainstorm" ideas (on her own if possible) in order to develop a *Wish List*. Often parents make the mistake of assuming that they know their child well enough to choose rewards for them without consultation. Don't make that mistake! Collaborating **with** your child in establishing a *Wish List* is essential in developing a motivating reward system.

After your child has developed her *Wish List*, go over it with her. Discuss the items on the list openly and honestly. Decide which requests are convenient and affordable for your family. It will be very helpful to create a spirit of cooperation by finding things that you and your child can agree on. However, it is absolutely your sole right to veto any idea that is not to your liking (the example that we use is Sally Sample's desire to have her nose pierced). If you are not sure whether you agree to a certain request, it is better to say "no" for the time being than to adopt a "we'll see" attitude.

There must be a concrete agreement regarding which rewards are acceptable, and which are not, **before** the plan goes into effect. Your input and suggestions may be very welcome at this point; feel free to offer ideas about rewards that your child has not considered.

Your completed list should consist of rewards that are both **desirable to your child and acceptable to you**. Although it will probably be revised several times, the first *Wish List* is very important in setting a positive tone.

The uses and importance of the *Weekly Chart* and *Contract* are also discussed. The point system will probably need to be revised over time, for balancing the points earned with the "prices" of the various rewards can be complicated. Be patient and take your time with this task; it will be well worth the effort.

We think that both you and your child will enjoy this process. It may even be fun, and can transform the process of managing trich into a truly collaborative experience.

• CHAPTER 7: PUTTING YOUR PLAN INTO ACTION

Here we go! This chapter is the one where your child will actually begin using her *Weekly Chart* and earning rewards. At this point you may want to ask her how you can be most helpful. This will give her the opportunity to give you feedback. She might say something like, "Please don't ask me if I pulled today." On the other hand she might say, "If you see me touching my hair, would you toss me a Koosh Ball?" Only she knows what she needs.

An area where your input may be especially important is in deciding where to put your charts, etc. They should be placed where they can be viewed easily, but not scrutinized by guests. The refrigerator door, a homework desk, a night table in your child's room, or the inside of her bedroom door would be a good choice. We recommend against placing the chart in a drawer, where it may be easily forgotten.

Even though it is called a *Weekly Chart*, it will need to be reviewed on a daily basis, especially during the first several weeks of the program. In general, it works best to establish a consistent time of day (e.g., before dinner, at bedtime, or after school) to go over the chart with your child. At that time you can count the number of points earned.

For the first few weeks, we recommend that your child receive daily rewards instead of saving her points for larger rewards. That way, after she counts up her points each day, she can have the satisfaction of reaping the benefits immediately. Most children need this level of reinforcement at the beginning of the program. Once the replacement behaviors are well established your child will be better able to delay gratification and can work towards medium or larger rewards. Modifications of this approach are discussed in the chapter.

When reviewing the *Weekly Chart* with your child, remember to focus on your child's use of **replacement behaviors, not on whether or how many hairs were pulled.** Once your child learns better management techniques, the hair pulling should diminish considerably, and the hair will have a chance to grow back. But the first step is to learn and use a variety of replacement behaviors that will substitute for or otherwise interfere with pulling. This is the key to success, so please help your child by emphasizing the importance of using her replacement behaviors.

This chapter also outlines how to implement your child's plan on a week by week basis. It is very likely that your child will need to revise her *Weekly Chart* every week for a while. That is to be expected, because every week your child will be increasing her awareness about her hair pulling behavior. This "new" information will need to be incorporated into the program, and changing the *Weekly Chart* is all part of the process. We encourage our clients to try using a variety of strategies and to discover which are useful and which are not. It is a process of learning and discovery, so try to be supportive and positive regarding your child's efforts, even when she goes through difficult weeks. You may want to offer suggestions during this process, but please do not get too upset if she does not always take your suggestions. We are urging her to become more independent, and making her own choices is part of the process.

• CHAPTER 8: HOLDING YOUR OWN

The information in this chapter is essentially that of "relapse prevention." As in previous steps, the role for the parent is a very delicate one. Sometimes your child may want a pep talk from you; other times she may simply want to be left alone. Either way, **slips will happen!** These slips are essential to learning problem solving and management skills.

If your child is emotionally distraught over a slip, then it will be more likely that her relapse will be more severe. On the other hand, if she is relatively calm and confident, her ability to use good problem solving strategies will be much more likely to occur, and the better her problem solving abilities, the more quickly she will be able to get back on track.

Your child's emotional state will be influenced by the emotional climate that you create. Maintaining a positive, or at least neutral, atmosphere will be extremely helpful to her at these times. We see your role at this point as that of a cheerleader and solid, confident source of support. If she gets off track, remind your child about the strategies that she has used that have been successful. Let her know that slips are part of the process. If asked, try to help your child by focusing on problem solving. Where did the slip happen? What was she doing? What might she do differently next time? These kinds of questions lead to better problem solving skills. Perhaps your child can work on anticipating the next possible slip. What might she do in order to minimize or even prevent that kind of slip to occur in the future? Remind her that the process is a long one, and that if she keeps on trying new things and using her strategies consistently, she should be able to gain more and more control over time. Encourage her to use her *Trichotillomania Review Form* to help her with the process.

There may be times when your child has difficulty but is unresponsive to your suggestions. It may be extremely difficult, but you may need to let your child "fall down" so that she can learn when she needs to ask for help. If you find yourself nagging or becoming intrusive, try to step back. Offering unsolicited advice and help will probably fall upon deaf ears. Try to be patient. Even when children have severe relapses, they are never back to square one. They can and will regain control when they are ready, and each time they get back on track they can use what they have previously learned to help them do better problem solving in the future.

• CHAPTER 9: LOOKING BACK AND PLANNING AHEAD

This chapter reviews the work that has been accomplished and discusses the importance of planning ahead for the future. We believe that by completing this program your child will be better able to manage trich for the rest of her life. However, your child may well have a predisposition for hair pulling, and therefore must always be aware that urges to pull hair may pop up "out of the blue." Remember that currently there is no cure for trich, so understanding that this vulnerability exists is essential for the ongoing successful management of this condition.

• CHAPTER 10: CONCLUSION: A FEW FINAL WORDS

The final chapter expresses the authors' confidence in your child and in her ability to use the problem solving skills that she has learned to manage trich. It also gives her the perspective that trich is only a small part of who she is as a person. Children (and even adults, at times) may lose perspective when it comes to coping with trich. It is important for your child to remember that while we sincerely hope that she will manage trich, and hopefully stop pulling her hair, she can live a full and productive life, whether or not she pulls her hair. We invite her to send us her comments and suggestions. We would very much like to hear from you, her parent, as well. Our address is noted at the end of this chapter.

QUESTIONS AND ANSWERS

Here are some of the most commonly asked questions that we usually receive and some answers that we hope will be helpful.

Q. *Why can't she just stop pulling?*

A. Trich is a very powerful and complex problem that in some cases may have a neurological basis. Even though it may not always seem so, almost all children truly want to be able to stop pulling their hair. But they can get easily frustrated when attempts to control their pulling have not been successful, and without adequate knowledge or skills, they may give up. Most likely, if your child could have easily stopped pulling her hair, she would have already done so!

Q. *Isn't this something my child will just outgrow?*

A. Hair pulling is not always a clinical problem. Tactile exploration is a normal part of development. If your child is hair pulling for a brief period of time (less than 3 months), or if your child is a preschooler and has not caused a great amount of damage, waiting may be the best approach in order to determine if a problem does indeed exist.

Here are some questions that you can ask yourself when trying to determine whether your child's hair pulling behavior has become a problem that you need to address:

- Has your child's hair pulling been consistent for more than three months?

- Is your child experiencing negative peer attention and/or is she bothered by the hair pulling?

- Has your child done considerable damage that is difficult to camouflage?

- Has hair pulling been incorporated into increasing numbers of activities?

- Has your child been unable to control or stop hair-pulling behavior, despite expressing a desire to do so?

If you answered "yes" to one or more of these questions it is time to approach the problem in a systematic way. This book can help. By following the steps of this program your child can gain a sense of control over this tenacious problem.

Q. *Should a mental health professional help us use this program?*

A. You and your child can go through the book together, or you may decide to seek out help from a professional, and have him or her lead you and your child through the program. Finding a therapist who has experience treating TTM may be difficult. Therefore, we recommend that you look for someone both you and your child feel comfortable with, and who is open to using this book as a guide.

Hair pulling not only effects your child; it effects you too. Because it may be extremely difficult to watch your child struggle with this complicated problem, it is crucial that you feel supported and guided. If reading this book does not provide enough support or if you find your child's hair pulling unbearable, it will be very important for you to speak with a mental health professional who can provide some parenting advice and guidance.

Q. *What if my child will not use this program or work with a mental health professional?*

A. Motivation and emotional readiness are essential for managing trich. The disorder may be more upsetting to you than it is for your child at the present time. While many children are able and even eager to work on managing trich, others may not be very concerned about their problem or their hair loss, and therefore may not be ready to work on managing their hair pulling problem. However upsetting your child's TTM is to you, remember that in the big picture, having trich is not the worst thing that can happen to a child, and it is not a life threatening illness that requires immediate intervention. If your child resists using this or other therapeutic child who is ready and motivated can make far more progress than one who is responding solely to parental pressure.

Q. *Won't the use of medications eliminate the hair pulling?*

A. As of yet, no single medication has been discovered that can reliably eliminate or even reduce hair pulling on a permanent basis. Because each person's hair pulling problem is unique, even if an effective drug were found tomorrow, it would not be right for everyone.

This does not mean that drugs are useless, however. While the search goes on for medications or combinations of medications that provide targeted relief of trichotillomania, a number of different varieties of drugs have been reported to be helpful for **some** people who pull their hair. Typically, these medications help by improving other conditions (such as depression, anxiety, or hyperactivity) that tend to exacerbate hair pulling.

The medications that are most often used in the treatment of TTM are anti-depressants commonly used in the treatment of Obsessive Compulsive Disorder. A host of other medications have also been tried, including mood stabilizers. In addition, stimulant medications, which are usually prescribed for Attention Deficit Disorder, have been tried. It should be mentioned, however, that these medications might have the unfortunate side effect of actually **increasing** hair pulling in some children. For some sufferers, hair pulling may be related to a type of tic disorder. In these cases, medications ordinarily prescribed for tics or Tourette's Disorder have been used.

As with any medication used to affect mood or behavior, it is extremely important to see a **psychiatrist who is experienced** in prescribing these medications and who can anticipate and manage some of the potential side effects.

For the majority of children who pull their hair, medication use is not necessary. Many children respond well to a comprehensive, well monitored cognitive-behavioral program, such as the one described in this book.

Q. *Will my child's hair ever grow back?*

A. Most likely, yes. The children with whom we have worked have all regained full heads of hair once they have learned to manage TTM. When pulling does not occur, the hair root is allowed to "rest," and hair growth can resume, although this may take up to several months. If you are concerned that some unusual medical condition may exist for your child that is interfering with hair growth, then we suggest that you consult your pediatrician or a dermatologist.

Q. *When my child's hair is growing in, should I say something about how nice it looks?*

A. The short answer to this question is, NO! Remember that we are focusing on the behavior, not the hair growth. If your child is successfully working with a variety of new techniques, then the hair will eventually grow in. However, the hair will not grow at a perfect rate, nor without some pulling episodes. Commenting on how pretty your child's hair looks on a particular day may lead her to feel worse following a hair pulling "slip." This may lead to increased pulling due to her frustration and disappointment in herself.

On the other hand, it's always a good idea to make positive and encouraging statements about how well your child has done with developing and using a variety of strategies and alternative behaviors. Noticing all of the hard work she has been doing, or commenting on how nicely she has been working on her management plan focuses on the behavior rather than the hair. These are positive, productive comments that will be meaningful to her, and that will help her get back on track when she slips.

Q. *What should I say to friends who ask about my child's hair?*

A. Ask your child what she would like people to know. This information may be accurate or a fabrication that will allow her to maintain some personal privacy. If your child is comfortable letting people know about the hair pulling, a short and simple explanation is best. "My child has developed a problem with hair pulling and we're getting help for it," is usually sufficient. If your child would like to maintain some privacy around this information, agreeing upon a plausible "explanation" would be most useful. Common explanations for hair loss include allergy problems, skin conditions, or dermatological problems, etc.

If you feel that you need support with this difficult parenting challenge, choose one or two close friends to confide in. Speaking with other adults and giving out additional information should be done only after discussing it with your child.

Q. *What if this book is not helping?*

A. Most children and adolescents are ill equipped to use a book like this one on their own, but they may not be willing to allow their parents to help them. Or, the parent and child may have conflicts when trying to work on this program together. In such cases, finding a therapist who is willing use this book as a therapeutic guide may be very important. It may not be easy to find someone willing to us this approach, but don't give up. The additional structure of going to a professional office and "reporting" to someone other than one's parents can be extremely helpful for some children.

Q. *Is my child's hair pulling my fault?*

A. NO! Just as you cannot take credit for your child's ability in ballet or lack of ability in soccer, you cannot take responsibility for you child's difficulty with hair pulling.

Some children have a genetic predisposition to hair pulling and through a unique set of circumstances end up pulling out their hair. Other children who **should** have a genetic predisposition to hair pulling **never pull their hair.** Other children have **no genetic** history of TTM at all, but pull their hair anyway. Most children who we have treated **do not have parents who have had trichotillomania.**

So, let yourselves off the hook! There was nothing that you could have or should have done differently that would have prevented your child's difficulty with hair pulling. The most important thing that you can do now is to learn how you can best help her to manage her problem.

CONCLUSION

We hope that this book has provided you and your child with the knowledge and tools needed to manage trichotillomania. We wish you the best of luck in your efforts!

If you would like to learn more about trichotillomania, we highly recommend that you contact the Trichotillomania Learning Center (TLC), 1215 Mission St., Suite 2, Santa Cruz, CA 95060. The telephone number is (831) 457-1004.

If you have any suggestions or comments about this book, please feel free to contact us. Our address is:

Ruth Golomb, M.Ed., LCPC and
Sherrie Vavrichek, LCSW-C

Writers' Cooperative of Greater Washington
P.O. Box 10550
Silver Spring, Maryland   20914-0550

APPENDIX

INFORMATION ABOUT MY PULLING CHECKLIST

1. Some people pull from a number of places on their bodies. Where on your body do you pull from?

I pull from my:

___ Head   ___ Eyelashes
___ Eyebrows   ___ Arms
___ Pubic Area   ___ Underarms
___ Legs   ___ Other _____

2. Some people pull mostly when they are in their own homes. Other people pull mostly outside of their homes. Still others pull equal amounts in and outside of the house.

I usually pull when I am:

In my house: **Outside of my house:**

___ Living room   ___ Classroom
___ Dining room   ___ Library
___ Family room   ___ Movie Theater
___ Rec room   ___ Car
___ Kitchen   ___ Other _____
___ Bathroom
___ Bedroom
___ Other _____

3. Many people pull with the help of some implement. Which, if any, of these do you use when you pull?

When I pull I sometimes use:

___ Mirror
___ Tweezers

4. Many people find that they pull while they are doing certain activities. Which of the following are likely to "trigger" hair pulling?

Doing my school work:

____ Desk/computer work
____ Studying/reading
____ Taking tests
____ Other _____

Transitions/making decisions:

____ Waking up in the morning
____ Deciding what to wear
____ Going to sleep
____ Other _____

Other:

____ Looking in the mirror
____ Leaning head on hand
____ Putting on make-up
____ Grooming (brushing hair, washing face, etc)

When my hands are not busy:

____ Talking on the phone
____ Lying in bed
____ Riding in the car
____ At the movies
____ Watching TV
____ Walking
____ Other _____

5.   Some people find that they pull when they experience certain emotions or internal states. What feelings are you having when you pull?

I pull when I feel:

____ Sad
____ Worried or afraid
____ Bored
____ Angry with others
____ Angry with myself
____ Frustrated

____ Unsure about what to do
____ Excited
____ Happy
____ Hungry
____ Tired
____ Other _____

6. Some kids mistakenly think (or hope) that something "magical" will happen when they pull.

I pull for these superstitious reasons:

____ Revenge
____ Getting rid of something bad

____ Luck
____ Other _____

7. Many people find that certain characteristics about certain hairs really bother them or are interesting to see or touch, so they might pull out those hairs. Sometimes people are also bothered by certain results of the hair pulling, so they may pull more hair in order to "even out" or "correct" the "mistake."

I pull when I:

___ See out of place hairs
___ See uneven growth
___ See dark/light hairs
___ Other _____

___ Touch sharp hairs
___ Touch short hairs
___ Touch thick hairs

8. Many people find that they have certain sensations when they pull.

When I pull:

___ It feels good
___ It hurts
___ It feels tingly/interesting
___ I like the way it feels when I bite or play with the follicle/hair
___ Other (Specify) _____

9. Some people will NOT pull in front of certain people, while others will pull in front of anyone.

I do NOT pull my hair in front of:

___ My parents
___ My brother(s)
___ My sister(s)
___ My friends

___ My classmates
___ My teacher
___ Strangers
___ Other _____

10. People do very different things with the hair once it has been pulled. After I pull hair out I:

___ Play with it	___ Throw it out
___ Bite it	___ Hide it
___ Swallow it*	___ Leave it in a pile
___ Flush it down the toilet	___ Other _____

(*Note: If you eat or swallow the hair, it can create serious health problems. Therefore it is very important that you tell your parents and see your doctor.)

11. Is there anything else about your habit that was not asked? If so, make a note of it below. Remember, you want to find out as much as possible about your habit so that you can come up with a really good plan!

Anything else about my pulling:

_____

PROBLEM SOLVING CHART

ACTIVITIES THAT TRIGGER PULLING

→ → → → → → → → → → → → → → → → → →

LOCATIONS → → →	Watching TV	Doing homework	Waiting for my turn to kick	Doing Xbox work
Bedroom				
Bathroom				
Living room	(H)Hot peppers (S) baseball	(H)wear bandaids (F) silly putty		
School			Fighting stance hands clenched	(F) grown (F) silly putty

F = **Fiddle** with hand and /or mouth alternatives

S = **Meet your body's Sensory** needs

H = Make it **Hard** to pull

E = Change your **Environment**

Em = Deal with your **Emotions** in a better way

P = Don't be **Perfectionistic**

WEEKLY CHART: Date Started _____

LOCATION/ACTIVITY	STRATEGY	POINTS	S	M	T	W	TH	F	S

Points Earned Today:									
+ **Balance Forward:**									
Subtotal:									
- Points Spent:									
NEW BALANCE:									

F = **Fiddle**
S = Meet your **Sensory** needs
H = Make it **Hard** to pull
E = **Change** your **Environment**
E(m) = Deal with your **Emotions** in a better way
P = Don't be **Perfectionistic**

The Hair Pulling Habit and You, Revised Edition, © 2000

WEEKLY CHART: Date Started _____

LOCATION/ACTIVITY	STRATEGY	POINTS	S	M	T	W	TH	F	S

Points Earned Today:	
+ Balance Forward:	
Subtotal:	
- Points Spent:	
NEW BALANCE:	

F = **Fiddle**
S = Meet your **Sensory** needs
H = Make it **Hard** to pull
E = Change your **Environment**
E(m) = Deal with your **Emotions** in a better way
P = Don't be **Perfectionistic**

WEEKLY CHART: Date Started _____

LOCATION/ACTIVITY	STRATEGY	POINTS	S	M	T	W	TH	F	S

Points Earned Today:				
+ Balance Forward:				
Subtotal:				
- Points Spent:				
NEW BALANCE:				

F = **Fiddle**
S = Meet your **Sensory** needs
H = Make it **Hard** to pull
E = Change your **Environment**
E(m) = Deal with your **Emotions** in a better way
P = Don't be **Perfectionistic**

The Hair Pulling Habit and You, Revised Edition, © 2000

WEEKLY CHART: Date Started _____

LOCATION/ACTIVITY	STRATEGY	POINTS	S	M	T	W	TH	F	S

Points Earned Today:	
+ Balance Forward:	
Subtotal:	
– Points Spent:	
NEW BALANCE:	

F = **Fiddle**
S = Meet your **Sensory** needs
H = Make it **Hard** to pull
E = Change your **Environment**
E(m) =Deal with your **Emotions** in a better way
P = Don't be **Perfectionistic**

WEEKLY CHART: Date Started _____

LOCATION/ACTIVITY	STRATEGY	POINTS	S	M	T	W	TH	F	S

Points Earned Today:	
+ Balance Forward:	
Subtotal:	
- Points Spent:	
NEW BALANCE:	

F = Fiddle
S = Meet your Sensory needs
H = Make it Hard to pull
E = Change your Environment
E(m) =Deal with your Emotions in a better way
P = Don't be Perfectionistic

WISH LIST

Small Rewards (can earn at least one every day):

Medium Rewards (can be earned in 4-7 days):

Large Rewards (can be earned in 2-4 weeks):

CONTRACT

I, _____, AGREE TO
TRY TO USE THE STRATEGIES ON MY WEEKLY
LIST. I WILL WRITE UP MY POINTS EVERY DAY IN
ORDER TO KEEP TRACK OF HOW I AM DOING.

MY PARENTS AGREE TO LET ME TRADE IN MY
POINTS FOR THE ITEMS ON MY WISH LIST.

_____

Signature   Date

_____

Parent Signature   Date

TRICH REVIEW FORM

Date _____

Here are the trigger situations (locations, times of day, and activities) where I am having problems:

_____

_____

By answering these questions I can help myself get back on track:

1) Is my *Problem-Solving Chart* up to date (does it include my current triggers)? _____ If not, what needs to be changed? _____

_____

2) Do I need to use my *Weekly Chart* more regularly? _____ Does it include my current trigger situations? _____ Am I keeping track of my points? _____

3) Does my *Weekly Chart* have enough different kinds of strategies? _____ . Note what they are and whether I am using them daily:

       Fiddling _____
       Sensory _____
       Habit _____
       Environment _____
       Emotion _____
       Perfectionism _____

4) Does my reward system need to be "beefed up"? _____ If so, how?

_____

5) What new strategies should I use and what supplies will I need to add to my baskets?_____

_____

6) The next time that I have the urge to pull, what should Ido to prevent an episode or at least minimize the damage? _____

_____

BIBLIOGRAPHY

Golomb, R.G., Mansueto, C.S., (1994). Trichotillomania in children. *In Touch. Newsletter of the Trichotillomania Learning Center*, 2, (8), 1, 6-7.

Mansueto, C.S., Golomb, R.G., Thomas, A.M., Stemberger, R.M., (1999). A comprehensive model for behavioral treatment of trichotillomania. *Cognitive and Behavioral Practice*, 6, 23-43.

Mansueto, C.S., Stemberger, R.M., Thomas, A.M., Golomb, R.G., (1997). Trichotillomania: A comprehensive behavioral model. *Clinical Review*, 17, 567-577.

Penzel, F., (2000). *Obsessive-Compulsive Disorders: A Complete Guide to Getting Well and Staying Well.* New York: Oxford University Press.

Salazar, C., (1995). *You Are Not Alone: Compulsive Hair Pulling "The Enemy Within."* Sacramento: Rophe Press.

Stein, D., Christenson, G., Hollander, E., (1999). Trichotillomania. Washington, D.C.: *American Psychiatric Press, Inc.*

ABOUT THE AUTHORS...

Ruth Goldfinger Golomb, M.Ed., LCPC, is a clinician and supervisor at the Behavior Therapy Center of Greater Washington, where she has been a staff member since the mid 1980's. During this time she has specialized in working with clients of all ages who suffer from anxiety disorders. Ms. Golomb has also been a co-investigator in a number of research projects regarding trichotillomania and obsessive compulsive disorder, and has co-authored several articles related to those studies. In addition, she has led a variety of workshops and training seminars on these and other topics for children, parents, educators, and mental health professionals. Ms. Golomb received her M.Ed. in counseling from the University of Maryland in 1985.

Sherrie Mansfield Vavrichek, LCSW-C, BCD, is a board certified clinical social worker who has served in medical, psychiatric, and special education settings in the Washington metropolitan area for over two decades . For the past ten years she has been on the staff at the Behavior Therapy Center of Greater Washington, where she works with children, teens, and adults suffering from a variety of psychological problems, including trichotillomania. Over the past several years, she has written about and conducted workshops on numerous topics, including trichotillomania, parenting issues, cognitive-behavior therapy, and the care of the special needs child. Ms. Vavrichek received her MSW from the University of Maryland School of Social Work in 1977.

Writers' Cooperative of Greater Washington
P.O. Box 10550
Silver Spring, Maryland 20914-0550